DICTIONARY OF
FIRST NAMES

DICTIONARY OF FIRST NAMES

Claremont Books
London

This edition published 1995 by Claremont Books,
an imprint of Godfrey Cave Associates,
42 Bloomsbury Street, London, WC1B 3QJ.

ISBN 1 85471 707 3

Printed in UK

CONTENTS

Introduction

In the modern world, each child is born with a compound name, consisting of a surname and a first name (or names), which provides an identity. The surname cannot be changed until the child reaches adult life, but the first name (or names) must be chosen by the parents, whether the choice be a completely free one, affected only by euphony, or limited for family or religious reasons.

When the human world was young, surnames did not exist. As witness in the Old Testament, a name was generally original, that is, given in the first instance to the individual bearing it, and either originating in some circumstance at birth or expressing some religious feeling, thus Jacob (supplanter), Isaiah (salvation of the Lord), Hannah (grace), Deborah (bee), and so on. Neither did the Hebrews, the Egyptians, the Assyrians, the Babylonians, the Persians nor the Greeks have surnames; and in the earliest period of their history the same can be said of the Romans.

In the course of time, however, every Roman citizen had three names: the *pronomen*, or personal name; the *nomen*, or name of the clan; and finally the *cognomen*, or family name, as, for example, Publius Cornelius Scipio. Conquerors were occasionally complimented by the addition of a fourth name, or *agnomen*, which commemorated their conquests, as, for example, Publius Cornelius Scipio Africanus.

Greek names refer to personal appearance or character, and were often supplemented by the occupation, place of birth, or a nickname. Times of great public excitement have had a very considerable influence in modifying the fashion in names. It is impossible to state with any degree of certainty when the modern system of personal nomenclature became general.

The early Germanic name was personally descriptive, a compound of a noun and an adjective: Arnold means strong as an eagle; Bernard, strong bear; Alfred, good or wise counsellor; Edmund, defender of happiness; Robert, bright in fame, and so on.

Early names have been changed and enlarged during the centuries and, with the gradual development of the surname, have evolved into that form, a practice which has now been turned round by the fashion for including surnames as first names.

In the Christian era, the name first given at Antioch has assumed the feminine forms of Christiana, Christina, and Chrissie; and in the male form Christopher, Kester, Kitt, Chris.

Richard runs the variations from Dick, Dickon, Dickson, Dickens, Dickonson, Dixon, Dix, through Hitch,

Hitchcock, Hitchcox, Hitchens, Higgs, Higgin, Higgins to Ricardo, Richards, Richley, Richman, Ritchie, and has therefore given rise to a large number of family names.

England, until the time of the Norman Conquest, knew no Scriptural names for English people, only Germanic names such as those which have already been quoted, for example Albert and Alfred. Any Biblical names in England before the Conquest are exclusively ecclesiastical titles. The introduction of Scriptural names into Normandy dates no earlier than a generation or two before the Conquest.

In the Domesday Book we still find no Philip, no Thomas, only one Nicholas, and very few Johns. By the end of the 14th century, however, John, William, Robert, and Thomas account for 80 per cent of the men in the Manors of Durham; and John, William, Thomas and Richard more than half the men in the West Riding of Yorkshire.

Names have always been subject to fashion. William the Conqueror set the name William in fashion in England; his son Robert, Robert; Thomas à Becket, Thomas; Richard I, Richard; Charles I, Charles; the Hanovers, George. After the Norman Conquest, Constance became a favourite feminine name, as Constance was the name of a daughter of William the Conqueror, of a daughter of Stephen, and of a daughter-in-law of Henry II, and, as with royalty, so with literature, became the heroine of Chaucer's *Man of Lawes* Tale. The name Juliana, also introduced into England with the Normans, suffered successive depreciation to Gilian, Gill or Jill. Curiously, Jack came to become inseparably coupled with Gill: "Each Jack shall have his Gill". In the *Townley Mysteries*, when Noah is pressing his wife to enter the ark, she still insists on putting in a little more spinning:

> "Sir, for Jak nor for Gille
> Will I turne my face
> Till I have on this hille
> Spun a space upon my rok" (distaff).

Into the 18th century, "gill" was a common byword for a flirt. The last stage of descent in the history of classical Juliana is registered in our "jilt". Juliet is a diminutive of Julia of Juliana. Juliet, further contracted into Juet, became Jowet in the north of England, from which the surname Jowett was derived. In the 14th and subsequent centuries, the ruling feminine names in England were Agnes, Alice, Joan, Margaret, Isabella, Cecilia, and Matilda. From the time of Charles I, the feminine names in order of popularity were Ann, Elizabeth, Jane, Margaret, Mary, Alice, Isabel, Dorothy, and Ellen.

Mary was first elevated into the Royal Court when a daughter of Edward I was named Marie, a circumstance ascribable to the influence of the Crusades. Robin Hood's maid was Marion, a diminutive of Mary. Mary occurs in English records in the diminutive form also of Mariot (Mariot Joscelyn, Mariota Gosebeck), which led to the surnames Mariott and Maryatt.

Among the earliest Biblical names adopted in England were John and Elizabeth. The Miracle Plays made Adam and Eve known, and these names were adopted in England. Adam appears in a diminutive form as Adekin (Adekin le Fuller), giving rise to the surnames Adkins, Adkinson, Atkinson, Addison. From Eve we have Eveson, Evett and Evitt. David has given birth to English surnames such as Davies, Davidson, Dawes, Dawson, Dawkes, Dawkins, Dawkinson, Dakins, etc.

Pilgrims bringing home with them each a bottle of water from the River Jordan in the Holy Land familiarized the name of Jordan, which flourished in England as Jordan and Judd. Elijah, again, is the prototype of the English Ellis, Elice, Ellice, Eliot, Elkin, Elkinson, Allison, etc.

Peter was the forerunner of Piers and Pierce. Simon, too, figures in England as Sim, Simkin, Sims, Simpson, Simmons, Simonds, Symonds. From Philip we derive our Philp, Philps, Phipps, Phipson, Philpotts, Phillots.

From Robert alone are derived no fewer than forty-six differently spelled surnames. Robin Hood, too, still names hundreds of country inns, and Robin also names birds, beasts, and shrubs. Also pet-named "Hob" or "Dob", he stands godfather to the *ignis fatuus,* as "Robin Goodfellow", "Hob-goblin", "Hob-lanthorn", "Hob-thrush".

In the Puritan era the use of abstract nouns as names took hold as well as the continuing use of Biblical names. The following are London Presbyterian entries: "1613, July 28. Baptised Jaell, daughter of Roger Mainwaring."

"1617, January 25. Baptised Ezekyell, sonne of Mr. Richard Culverwell".

Girl babies of the same period were baptised Priscilla, Dorcas, Tabitha, Martha, Rebecca, and Deborah. Within a few pages of the West Riding Directory of the early 17th century, were found three Pharaohs, three Hephzibahs (on one single page), "Adah and Zillah Pickle, milliners"; "Jehoiada Rhodes, maker of saws"; "Barzillai Williamson, butcher"; "Jachin Firth" (taking his first name somewhere out of *Kings*) "beer retailer"; and Shadrach, Meshach, and Abednego all serve in this directory as "Christian" names. Other entries are Azariah Griffiths, Naphtali Matson, Philemon Jakes, Malachi Ford, Shallum Richardson.

In the *Sussex Archæological Collections* is the following entry of baptism:

"1630, November 18. Baptised Humiliation, son of Humiliation Hinde". This son dying, the father seven years later has another Humiliation to fill the vacant place: "1637-8, January 21. Baptised Humiliation, son of Humiliation Hinde".

Among the numerous family of the patriarchal pilgrim Roger Clap (who died in Boston, Massachusetts in 1691), there were three sons named Preserved, Hopestill, and Desire, and a daughter, Wait.

Dr Increase Mather was sent from New England to convey to James II. the thanks of the Dissenters for a Toleration Act in 1685.

The following names can be found in the registers of Warbleton: 1617, Bestedfast Elyarde, Goodgift Gynnings; 1622, Lament Willard; 1625, Faint-not Dighurst, Fere-not Rhodes; 1677, Replenish French.

A late survival or restoration of Puritan names is reported in *Notes and Queries*, September 9, 1865:—

"A man named Sykes, resident in this locality (Thrustonland, West Riding, Yorkshire), had four sons whom he named respectively Love-well, Do-well, Die-well, and the youngest Fare-well. Sad to say, Fare-well Sykes met an untimely end by drowning, and was buried this week (11th Sunday after Trinity) in Lockwood churchyard. The brothers Live-well, Do-Well, and Die-well were the chief mourners on the occasion."

The intention nowadays in naming a child is not quite so lofty, and personal passions have been indulged: more than one child has been named after all the members of a football team.

Although the trend now is to choose a name because it sounds well, it is always wise to consider the meaning of the word. But whether the purpose is to find help or inspiration in "naming baby" or one of mere curiosity, this volume provides a basic listing of names and their meanings, origins and derives.

A

Aaron *masc* mountaineer, enlightener (*Hebrew*); a contracted dimunitive is **Arn**.

Abbie, Abby *fem* diminutive *forms* of **Abigail**, also used independently.

Abbott *masc* a surname, meaning father of the abbey, used as a first name (*Old English*).

Abe *masc* father (*Aramaic*); diminutive of **Abraham, Abram**.

Abel *masc* breath, fickleness, vanity (*Hebrew*).

Abelard *masc* nobly resolute (*Germanic*).

Abiathar *masc* father of plenty or excellence (*Hebrew*).

Aberah *fem* a variant form of **Averah**.

Abiel *masc* father of strength (*Hebrew*).

Abigail *fem* my father's joy (*Hebrew*); diminutive forms are **Abbie, Abby, Gail**.

Abihu *masc* to whom Jehovah is a father (*Hebrew*).

Abijah *masc* to whom Jehovah is a father (*Hebrew*); a diminutive form is **Bije**.

Abner *masc* father of light (*Hebrew*).

Abra *fem* mother of multitudes (*Hebrew*).

Abraham *masc* father of a multitude (*Hebrew*); diminutive forms are **Abe, Bram**.

Abram *masc* father of elevation (*Hebrew*); diminutive forms are **Abe, Bram**.

Absalom *masc* father of peace (*Hebrew*).

Acacia *fem* the name of a plant, possibly meaning immortality and resurrection, used as a first name (*Greek*).

Acantha *fem* thorny, spiney (*Greek*).

Ace *masc* unity, unit (*Latin*).

Ackerley *masc* a surname, meaning from the acre meadow, used as a first name (*Old English*).

Ackley *masc* a surname, meaning from the oak tree meadow, used as a first name (*Old English*).

Ada *fem* diminutive of **Adela** or names beginning with *Adal*, also used independently; a variant form of **Adah**.

Adabelle *fem* joyful and beautiful, a combination of **Ada** and **Belle**; variant forms are **Adabel, Adabela, Adabella**.

Adah *fem* adorning (*Hebrew*); variant forms are **Ada**.

Adair *masc* a Scottish form of **Edgar**.

Adalard *masc* noble and brave (*Germanic*).

Adalia *fem* an early Saxon tribal name whose origin is unknown (*Germanic*).

Adam *masc* man, earth man, red earth (*Hebrew*).

Adamina *fem* of Adam. (*Latin*);

Adar *fem* fire; as the name in the Jewish calendar for the twelfth month of the Biblical year and the sixth month of the civil year, it is a name sometimes given to girls born in that period (*Hebrew*).

Addie *fem* diminutive of **Adelaide**.

Addie, Addy, Mina.

Addison *masc* a surname, meaning Adam's son, used as a first name (*Old English*).

Adela *fem* of noble birth; a princess (*Germanic*).

Adelaide *fem* of noble birth; a princess (*Germanic*); a diminutive form is **Addie**.

Adelbert *see* **Albert**.

Adèle, Adele *fem* the French form of Adela, now also used as an English form.

Adelheid *fem* noble kind (*Germanic*); a diminutive form is **Heidi**.

Adeline, Adelina *fem* of noble birth; a princess (*Germanic*); a diminutive form is **Aline**.

Adelphia *fem* sisterly, eternal friend of mankind (*Greek*); variant forms are **Adelfia, Adelpha**.

Adin *masc* sensual (*Hebrew*).

Adina *fem* voluptuous, ripe, mature (*Hebrew*).

Adlai *masc* God is just (*Hebrew*).

Adler *masc* eagle, perceptive one (*Germanic*).

Adney *masc* island-dweller (*Old English*).

Adolf *masc* the German form of **Adolph**.

Adolph, Adolphus *masc* noble wolf; noble hero (*Germanic*); a diminutive form is **Dolph**.

Adolpha *fem* noble she-wolf, she who will give her life for her young, the *fem* form of Adolf (*Germanic*); variant forms are **Adolfa, Adolfina, Adolphina**.

Adolphe *masc* the French form of **Adolph**.

Adon, Adonai *masc* lord, a sacred word for God (*Hebrew*).

Adonia *fem* beautiful goddess of the resurrection; eternal renewal of youth (*Greek*).

Adoniram *masc* lord of height (*Hebrew*).

Adora *fem* adored and beloved gift (*Latin*).

Adorabella *fem* beautiful gift, a combination of **Adora** and **Bella**.

Adorna *fem* adorned with jewels (*Latin*).

Adrian *masc* of the Adriatic in Italy (*Latin*); a variant form is **Hadrian**.

Adrianne, Adrienne *fem* forms of **Adrian**.

Adriel *masc* from God's congregation (*Hebrew*).

Aefa *fem* a variant form of **Aoife**.

Aeneas *masc* commended (*Greek*); a variant form is **Eneas**.

Aethelbert *see* **Ethelbert**.

Aethelred *see* **Ethelred**.

Afonso *masc* the Portugese form of **Alphonso**.

Afra *fem* a variant form of **Aphra**.

Africa *fem* the name of the continent used as a first name.

Agatha *fem* good; kind (*Greek*); a diminutive form is **Aggie, Aggy, Nessa, Nessie**.

Agave *fem* illustrious, famous (*Greek*).

Aggie, Aggy *fem* diminutive forms of **Agatha, Agnes**.

Agnes *fem* chaste; pure (*Greek*); diminutive forms are **Aggie, Aggy**.

Agnès *fem* the French form of **Agnes**.

Agnese *fem* the Italian form of **Agnes**.

Agostino *masc* the Italian form of **Augustine**.

Agustín *masc* the Spanish form of **Augustine**.

Ahern *masc* horse lord, horse owner (*Irish Gaelic*).

Ahren *masc* eagle (*Germanic*).

Aidan *masc* fire, flame (*Irish Gaelic*); a variant form is **Edan**.

Aiken *masc* the Scottish form of **Atkin**, a surname meaning son of Adam, used as a first name (*Old English*).

Ailean *fem* Scots Gaelic form of **Alan**.

Aileen *fem* a variant form of **Eileen**.

Ailsa *fem* fairy (*Scots Gaelic*).

Aimée *fem* the French form of **Amy**.

Áine *fem* an Irish Gaelic form of **Anna**.

Ainsley *masc* a surname, meaning meadow of the respected one, used as a first name (*Old English*).

Ainslie *masc* a Scottish form of **Ainsley**, used as a first name.

Aisleen, Aisling *fem* vision (*Irish Gaelic*).

Al *masc* diminutive of **Alan, Albert**, etc.

Alain *masc* the French form of **Alan**.

Alan *masc* meaning uncertain, possibly a hound (*Slavonic*), harmony (*Celtic*); variant forms are **Allan, Allen**.

Alana, Alanna, Alannah *fem* forms of **Alan**; a variant form is **Lana**.

Alard *masc* a variant form of **Allard**.

Alaric *masc* noble ruler; all-rich (*Germanic*).

Alarice *fem* of **Alaric** (*Germanic*); variant forms are **Alarica, Alarise**.

Alasdair, Alastair *masc* variant forms of **Alister**.

Alban *masc* of Alba in Italy (*Latin*).

Albern *masc* noble warrior (*Old English*).

Albert *masc* all-bright; illustrious (*Germanic*); diminutive forms are **Al, Bert, Bertie**.

Alberta *fem* form of **Albert**.

Albin *see* **Alban**.

Albina *fem* white, very fair (*Latin*);.variant forms are **Albinia, Alvina, Aubina, Aubine**.

Albrecht *masc* a German form of **Albert**.

Alcina *fem* strong-minded one, from a legendary woman who could make gold from stardust (*Greek*).

Alcott *masc* the surname, meaning old cottage or hut, used as a first name (*Old English*).

Alcyone *fem* in Greek mythology a woman who drowned herself from grief at her husband's death and who was turned into a kingfisher; variant forms are **Halcyone, Halcyon**.

Alda *fem* wise and rich (*Germanic*); variant forms are **Eada, Elda**.

Alden *masc* a surname, meaning old or trustworthy friend, used as a first name (*Old English*).

Alder *masc* a surname, meaning alder tree, used as a first name (*Old English*); old, wise and rich (*Germanic*).

Aldis *masc* a surname, meaning old house, used as a first name (*Old English*); *fem* a diminutive of some names beginning with *Ald-*.

Aldo, Aldous *masc* old (*Germanic*).

Aldora *fem* of noble rank (*Old English*); variant forms are **Aelda, Aeldra**.

Aldrich *masc* a surname, meaning old, wise ruler, used as a first name (*Old English*).

Aldwin *see* **Alvin**.

Alec, Aleck *masc* diminutive *forms* of **Alexander**.

Aled *masc* the name of a river used as a first name (*Welsh*).

Aleria *fem* like an eagle (*Latin*).

Aleron *masc* eagle (*Latin*).

Alethea *fem* truth (*Greek*).

Alex *masc* diminutive of **Alexander**; *fem* diminutive of **Alexandra**, now both used independently; a variant form is **Alix**.

Alexa *fem* diminutive of **Alexandra**.

Alexander *masc* a helper of men (*Greek*); diminutive forms are **Alec, Alex, Alick, Lex, Sandy**.

Alexandra, Alexandrina *fem* forms of **Alexander**; diminutive forms are **Alex, Alexa, Lexie, Lexy, Sandie, Sandra, Sandy**.

Alexia *fem* form of **Alexis**.

Alexina *fem* form of **Alexander**.

Alexis *masc fem* help; defence (*Greek*).

Alf, Alfie *masc* diminutive forms of **Alfred**.

Alfonsine *fem* form of **Alphonse** (*Germanic*); variant forms are **Alphonsina, Alphonsine, Alphonza**.

Alfonso *masc* a Spanish and Italian form of **Alphonso**.

Alford *masc* a surname, meaning old ford, used as a first name (*Old English*).

Alfred *masc* good or wise counsellor (*Germanic*); diminutive forms are **Alf, Alfie**.

Alfreda *fem* form of **Alfred**; diminutive forms are **Alfie, Allie**; variant forms are **Elfreda, Elfreida, Elfrieda, Elfrida, Elva, Elga, Freda**.

Alger *masc* elf spear (*Old English*).

Algernon *masc* whiskered (*Norman French*); a diminutive form is **Algie, Algy**.

Alice, Alicia *fem* of noble birth; a princess (*Germanic*).— variant forms are **Alys, Alyssa**.

Alick *masc* diminutive of **Alexander**, now sometimes used independently.

Alida *fem* little bird; small and lithe (*Latin*); a Hungarian form of **Adelaide**; variant forms are **Aleda, Aleta, Alita**; diminutive forms are **Leda, Lita**.

Aliénor *fem* a French form of **Eleanor**.

Alima *fem* learned in music and dancing (*Arabic*).

Aline *fem* a contraction of **Adeline**.

Alison *fem* diminutive of **Alice**, now used entirely in its own right; a variant form is **Allison**; diminutive forms are **Allie, Ally**; *masc* son of Alice; son of a nobleman (*Old English*).

Alister *masc* the Scots Gaelic form of **Alexander**; variant forms are **Alasdair, Alastair**.

Alix *fem* a variant form of **Alex**.

Allan, Allen *masc* variant forms of **Alan**.

Allard *masc* noble and brave (*Old English*); a variant form is **Alard**,

Allegra *fem* a word for cheerful or blithe used as a first name (*Italian*).

Allie, Ally *fem* diminutive of **Alice, Alison**.

Allison *fem* a variant form of **Alison**.

Allison, Al, Allie.

Alloula, Allula, Aloula.

Alma *fem* loving, nurturing (*Latin*).

Almira *fem* lofty; a princess (*Arabic*).

Almo *masc* noble and famous (*Old English*).

Aloha *fem* a word for welcome used as a first name (*Hawaiian*).

Alonso *masc* a Spanish form of **Alphonso**; a diminutive form is **Lonnie**.

Alonzo *see* **Alphonso**.

Aloysius *masc* a Latin form of **Lewis**.

Alpha *masc, fem* first one (*Greek*).

Alpheus *masc* exchange (*Hebrew*).

Alphonse *masc* the French form of **Alphonso**.

Alphonso, Alphonsus *masc* all-ready; willing (*Old German*).

Alpin *masc* blond (*Scottish Gaelic*).

Alroy *masc* red-haired (*Scottish Gaelic*).

Alston *masc* a surname, meaning old stone, used as a first name (*Old English*).

Alta *fem* tall in spirit (*Latin*).

Althea *fem* a healer (*Greek*); a diminutive form is **Thea**.

Altman *masc* old, wise man (*Germanic*).

Alton *masc* a surname, meaning old stream or source, used as a first name (*Old English*).

Alula *fem* winged one (*Latin*); first (*Arabic*).

Alun *masc* the Welsh form of **Alan**.

Alura *fem* divine counsellor (*Old English*).

Alva *fem* white (*Latin*).

Alva *see* **Alban**.

Alvah *masc* exalted one (*Hebrew*).

Alvin, Alwin *masc* winning all (*Old English*).

Alvina, Alvine *fem* beloved and noble friend (*Germanic*); a diminutive form is **Vina**.

Alys, Alyssa *fem* variant forms of **Alice, Alicia**.

Alyth *fem* a placename, meaning steep place, used as a first name.

Alzena *fem* woman, purveyor of charm and virtue (*Arabic*).

Amabel *fem* lovable (*Latin*); a diminutive form is **Mabel**.

Amadea *fem* form of **Amadeus**.

Amadeus *masc* lover of God (*Latin*).

Amado *masc* the Spanish form of **Amato**.

Amalia *fem* work (*Germanic*); an Italian and Greek form of **Amelia**.

Amanda *fem* worthy of love (*Latin*); diminutive forms are **Manda, Mandy**.

Amariah *masc* whom Jehovah promised (*Hebrew*).

Amasa *masc* a burden (*Hebrew*).

Amber *fem* the name of a gemstone used as a first name.

Ambert *masc* shining bright light (*Germanic*).

Ambrogio *masc* the Italian form of **Ambrose**.

Ambrose *masc* immortal; divine (*Greek*).

Ambrosine *fem* form of Ambrose; variant forms are **Ambrosia, Ambrosina**.

Amédée *masc* the French form of **Amadeus**.

Amelia *fem* busy, energetic (*Germanic*); a diminutive form is **Millie**.

Amélie *fem* the French form of **Amelia**.

Amelinda *fem* beloved and pretty (*Spanish*); variant forms are **Amalinda, Amelinde**.

Amena *fem* honest, truthful (*Gaelic*).

Amerigo *masc* an Italian variant form of **Enrico**.

Amery *masc* a variant form of **Amory**.

Amethyst *fem* the name of the semi-precious gemstone used as a first name (*Greek*).

Aminta, Amintha, Aminthe *fem* protector, a shepherdess in Greek mythology (*Greek*).

Ammon *masc* hidden (*Egyptian*).

Amory *masc* famous ruler (*Germanic*); variant forms are **Amery, Emery, Emmery**.

Amos *masc* strong, courageous; a burden (*Hebrew*).

Amy *fem* beloved (*Old French*).

Anastasia *fem* rising up, resurrection (*Greek*); diminutive forms are **Stacey, Stacy, Stacie, Stasia**.

Anastasius *masc* form of **Anastasia**.

Anatholia, Anatola *fem* forms of Anatole (*Greek*; a variant form is **Anatolia**.

Anatole *masc* from the East (*Greek*).

Anatolia *fem* a variant form of **Anatholia**.

Andie *masc* diminutive of **Andrew**.

André *masc* the French form of **Andrew**, becoming popular as an English-language form.

Andrea *fem* form of **Andreas** or **Andrew**; a variant form is **Andrina**; *masc* the Italian form of **Andrew**.

Andreas *masc* Greek, Latin, and German forms of **Andrew**.

Andrés *masc* the Spanish form of **Andrew**.

Andrew *masc* strong; manly; courageous (*Greek*); diminutive forms are **Andie, Andy, Dandie, Drew**.

Andrina, Andrine *fem* variant forms of **Andrea**.

Aneirin, Aneurin *masc* noble, modest (*Welsh*); a diminutive form is **Nye**.

Anemone *fem* windflower, the name of the garden plant used as a first name (*Greek*).

Angel *fem* diminutive of **Angela** (*Greek*); *masc* form of **Angela**.

Angela, Angelina messenger (*Greek*).

Angelica *fem* lovely; angelic (*Greek*).

Angelo *masc* Italian form of **Angel**.

Angharad *fem* much loved (*Welsh*).

Angus *masc* excellent virtue (*Gaelic*); a diminutive form is **Gus**.

Anita *fem* Spanish diminutive of **Ann**, now used independently as an English-language form; a diminutive form is **Nita**.

Ann *fem* grace (*Hebrew*); a variant form is **Hannah**; a diminutive form is **Annie**.

Anna *fem* the Latin form of **Ann**.

Annabel, Annabelle, Annabella *fem* lovable (possibly from **Amabel**); diminutive forms are **Bella, Belle**.

Annan *masc* a Scottish placename, meaning water or waters, used as a first name (*Scottish Gaelic*).

Anne *fem* the French form of **Ann**.

Anneka *fem* a Dutch diminutive of **Anna**.

Annette *fem* a French diminutive of **Ann**, used as an English-language form.

Annika *fem* a Swedish diminutive of **Anna**.

Annis, Annice *fem* a medieval diminutive of **Agnes**.

Annona *fem* a variant form of **Anona**.

Annunciata *fem* Italian form of *nuntius*, bringer of news, i.e. the angel Gabriel, who delivered the announcement of the Virgin Mary's conception, a name often given to children born on 25 March, Lady Day (*Latin*).

Anona *fem* annual crops, hence the Roman goddess of crops (*Latin*); a variant form is **Annona**; diminutives are **Nonnie, Nona**.

Anora *fem* light, graceful (*Old English*).

Anscom *masc* one who dwells in a secret valley; a solitary person (*Old English*).

Anselm, Ansel *masc* a surname, meaning, god helmet, i.e. under the protection of God, used as a first name (*Germanic*).

Anselma *fem* form of **Anselm**; a variant form is **Arselma**.

Ansley *masc* a surname, meaning clearing with a hermitage or solitary dwelling, used as a first name (*Old English*).

Anson *masc* a surname, meaning son of Agnes or Anne, used as a first name (*Old English*).

Anstice *masc* a surname, meaning resurrected, used as a first name (*Greek*).

Anthea *fem* flowery (*Greek*).

Anthony *masc* a variant form of **Antony**; a diminutive form is **Tony**.

Antoine *masc* the French form of **Anthony**, now used independently as an English-language form; a variant form is **Antwan**.

Antoinette *fem* diminutive of **Antonia**, now used as an English-language form; a diminutive form is **Toinette**.

Anton *masc* a German form of **Antony**, now used as an English-language form.

Antonia *fem* form of **Antony**; diminutive forms are **Toni, Tonia, Tonie, Tony**.

Antonio *masc* the Italian and Spanish form of **Antony**.

Antony *masc* priceless; praiseworthy (*Latin*); a variant form is **Anthony**; a diminutive form is **Tony**.

Antwan *masc* a variant form of **Antoine**.

Anwell *masc* beloved (*Gaelic*).

Anwen *fem* very beautiful (*Welsh*).

Anyon *masc* anvil (*Gaelic*).

Aoife *fem* the Irish Gaelic form of **Eve**; a variant form is **Aefa**.

Aonghas *masc* Scots Gaelic form of **Angus**.

Aphra *fem* dust (*Hebrew*); woman from Carthage (*Latin*).—a variant form is **Afra**.

April *fem* the name of the month, *Aprilis*, used as a personal name (*Latin*).

Ara *fem* spirit of revenge, and the goddess of destruction and vengeance (*Greek*).

Arabella, Arabela *fem* a fair altar (*Latin*); a woman (*Arabic*); diminutive forms are **Bella, Belle**.

Araminta *fem* beautiful, sweet-smelling flower (*Greek*); a diminutive form is **Minta**.

Archard *masc* sacred and powerful (*Germanic*).

Archer *masc* a surname, meaning professional or skilled bowman, used as a first name (*Old English*).

Archibald *masc* very bold; holy prince (*Germanic*); diminutive forms are **Archie, Archy**.

Ardath *fem* field of flowers (*Hebrew*); variant forms are **Aridatha, Ardatha**.

Ardal *masc* high valour (*Irish Gaelic*).

Ardella, Ardelle, Ardelis *fem* enthusiasm, warmth (*Hebrew*).

Arden *masc* a surname, meaning dwelling place or gravel or eagle valley, used as a surname (*Old English*); burning, fiery (*Latin*).

Ardley *masc* from the domestic meadow (*Old English*).

Ardolph *masc* home-loving wolf rover (*Old English*).

Areta, Aretha *fem* excellently virtuous (*Greek*); variant forms are **Aretta, Arette**.

Argenta, Argente, Argente *fem* silver or silvery coloured (*Latin*).

Aretta, Arette *fem* variant forms of **Areta**.

Argus *masc* all-seeing, watchful one, from Argus Panoptes, a character from Greek mythology with a hundred eyes all over his body (*Greek*).

Argyle, Argyll *masc* the Scottish placename, meaning land or district of the Gaels, used as a first name (*Scots Gaelic*).

Aria *fem* the Italian word for beautiful melody, from *aer*, 'breeze' (*Latin*), used as a first name.

Ariadne *fem* very holy (*Greek*).

Arianna *fem* an Italian form of **Ariadne**.

Arianne *fem* a French form of **Ariadne**.

Aric *masc* sacred ruler (*Old English*); diminutive forms are **Rick, Rickie, Ricky**.

Ariel *masc* God's lion (*Hebrew*).

Ariella, Arielle *fem* forms of Ariel (*Hebrew*).

Aries *masc* the ram, the sign of the Zodiac for 21 March to 19 April (*Latin*).

Arlen *masc* pledge (*Irish Gaelic*).

Arlene *fem* form of Arlen; a variant form of **Charlene, Marlene**; variant forms are **Arleen, Arlena, Arlina, Arline, Arlyne**.

Arlie, Arley, Arly *masc* a surname, meaning eagle wood, used as a first name (*Old English*).

Armand *masc* a French form of **Herman**.

Armel *masc* stone prince or chief (*Breton Gaelic*).

Armelle *fem* form of Armel.

Armilla *fem* bracelet (*Latin*).

Armin *masc* military man (*Germanic*).

Armina, Armine *fem* forms of **Armin**; variant forms are **Erminie, Erminia**.

Armstrong *masc* a surname, meaning strong in the arm, used as a first name (*Old English*).

Arn *masc* diminutive of **Arnold, Arnulf**; a contraction of **Aaron**.

Arnalda *fem* form of **Arnold** (*Germanic*).

Arnall *masc* a surname variant form of **Arnold** used as a first name (*Germanic*).

Arnaud, Arnaut *masc* French forms of **Arnold**.

Arnatt, Arnett *masc* surname variant forms of **Arnold** used as first names.

Arne *masc* eagle (*Old Norse*); a diminutive form is **Arnie**.

Arno *masc* a diminutive of **Arnold, Arnulf**.

Arnold *masc* strong as an eagle (*Germanic*); eagle meadow (*Old English*); diminutive forms are **Arn, Arnie, Arno, Arny**.

Arnott *masc* a surname variant form of **Arnold** used as a first name.

Arnulf *masc* eagle wolf (*Germanic*); diminutives are **Arn, Arno**.

Arpad *masc* a variant form of **Arvad**.

Arselma *fem* a variant form of **Anselma**.

Artemas *masc* form of **Artemis** (*Greek*).

Artemis *fem* the name of the virgin Greek goddess of hunting and the moon, the derivation of which is unknown. The Roman equivalent is Diana.

Arthur *masc* high; noble (*Celtic*); a diminutive form is **Art**.

Arturo *masc* the Italian and Spanish forms of **Arthur**.

Arundel *masc* the English placename, meaning a valley where nettles grow, used as a first name (*Old English*).

Arva *fem* ploughed land, pasture (*Latin*).

Arvad *masc* wanderer (*Hebrew*); a variant form is **Arpad**.

Arval, Arvel *masc* greatly lamented (*Latin*).

Arvid *masc* eagle wood (*Norse*).

Arvin *masc* people's friend (*Germanic*).

Arwel *masc* meaning uncertain (*Welsh*).

Arwenna *fem* form of **Arwyn**.

Arwyn *masc* muse (*Welsh*); a variant form is **Awen**.

Asa *masc* healer, physician (*Hebrew*).

Asahel *masc* made of God (*Hebrew*).

Asaph *masc* a collector (*Hebrew*).

Ascot, Ascott *masc* an English placename and surname, meaning eastern cottages, used as a first name (*Old English*).

Ashburn *masc* a surname, meaning stream where the

ash trees grow, used as a first name (*Old English*).

Ashby *masc* an English placename, meaning ash-tree farmstead, used as a first name (*Old English*).

Asher *masc* happy, fortunate (*Hebrew*).

Ashford *masc* an English placename, meaning ford by a clump of ash trees, used as a first name (*Old English*).

Ashley, Ashleigh *masc, fem* the surname, meaning ash wood or glade, used as a first name (*Old English*).

Ashlin *masc* ash-surrounded pool (*Old English*).

Ashton *masc* an English placename, meaning ash-tree farmstead, used as a first name (*Old English*).

Ashur *masc* martial, warlike (*Semitic*).

Asphodel *fem* a daffodil-like plant, the origin of whose name is obscure, used as a first name (*Greek*).

Astra *fem* diminutive of **Astrid**.

Astrid *fem* fair god (*Norse*); a diminutive is **Astra**.

Atalanta, Atalante *fem* the name of a mythological character who agreed to marry the man who could outrun her (*Greek*); a variant form is **Atlanta**.

Atalya *fem* guardian (*Spanish*).

Athanasius *masc* immortal (*Greek*).

Athena, Ahthene, Athenée *fem* in Greek mythology, the goddess of wisdom. Her Roman counterpart is Minerva (*Greek*).

Atherton *masc* a surname, meaning noble army's place, used as a first name (*Old English*).

Athol, Atholl *masc* a placename and surname, meaning new Ireland, used as a first name (*Scots Gaelic*).

Atlante *fem* a variant form of **Atalanta**.

Atlee, Atley, Atley *masc* a surname, meaning at the wood or clearing, used as a first name (*Old English*).

Atwater, Atwatter *masc* a surname, meaning by the water, used as a first name (*Old English*).

Atwell *masc* a surname, meaning at the spring or well of, used as a first name (*Old English*).

Auberon *masc* noble bear (*Germanic*); a variant form is **Oberon**; a diminutive form is **Bron**.

Aubin *masc* a surname, meaning blond one, used as a first name (*French*).

Aubrey *masc* ruler of spirits (*Germanic*).

Audrey *fem* noble might (*Old English*).

August *masc* the Polish and German form of **Augustus**; the eighth month of the year, named after the Roman emperor **Augustus**, used as a first name.

Augusta *fem* form of **Augustus**; diminutive forms are **Gussie, Gusta**.

Auguste *masc* the French form of **Augustus**.

Augustin *masc* the German and French forms of **Augustine**.

Augustine *masc* belonging to **Augustus** (*Latin*); a diminutive form is **Gus**.

Augustus *masc* exalted; imperial (*Latin*); a diminutive form is **Gus**.

Aura, Aure, Aurea *fem* breath of air (*Latin*); a variant form is **Auria**.

Aurelia *fem* form of **Aurelius**.

Aurelius *masc* golden (*Latin*).

Auria *fem* a variant form of **Aura**.

Aurora *fem* morning redness; fresh; brilliant (*Latin*).

Austin *masc* a contraction of **Augustine**.

Autumn *fem* the name of the season, the origin of which is uncertain, used as a first name.

Ava *fem* origin uncertain, perhaps a Germanic diminutive of names beginning *Av*.

Avera *fem* transgressor (*Hebrew*); a variant form is **Aberah**.

Averil, Averill *fem* English forms of **Avril**.

Avery *masc* a surname, derived from **Alfred**, used as a surname (*Old English*).

Avice, Avis *fem* possibly bird (*Latin*).

Avril *fem* the French form of **April**.

Awen *masc* a variant form of **Arwyn**.

Axel *masc* father of peace (*Germanic*).

Axton *masc* stone of the sword fighter (*Old English*).

Aylmer *masc* a surname, meaning noble and famous, used as a first name (*Old English*).

Aylward *masc* a surname, meaning noble guardian, used as a first name (*Old English*).

Azaliea, Azalia, Azalee *fem* variant forms of the name of the azalea plant, supposed to prefer dry earth, used as a first name.

Azaria *fem* form of **Azarias**.

Azarias *masc* helped by God (*Hebrew*).

Azura, Azure *fem* blue as the sky (*French*).

B

Bab, Babs *fem* diminutive forms of **Barbara**.

Bailey, Baillie *masc* a surname, meaning bailiff or steward, used as a first name (*Old French*); a variant form is **Bayley**.

Bainbridge *masc* a surname, meaning bridge over a short river, used as a first name (*Old English*).

Baird *masc* a Scottish surname, meaning minstrel or bard, used as a first name (*Celtic*); a variant form is **Bard**.

Baldemar *masc* bold and famous prince (*Germanic*).

Baldovin *masc* the Italian form of **Baldwin**.

Baldric, Baldrick *masc* a surname, meaning princely or bold ruler, used as a first name (*Germanic*); a variant form is **Baudric**.

Baldwin *masc* bold friend (*Germanic*).

Balfour *masc* a surname from a Scottish placename, meaning village with pasture, used as a first name (*Scots Gaelic*).

Ballard *masc* a surname, meaning bald, used as a first name (*Old English, Old French*).

Balthasar, Balthazar *masc* Baal defend the king (*Babylonian*).

Bambi *fem* a variant form of the word for *bambino*, child (*Italian*).

Bancroft *masc* a surname, meaning bean place, used as a first name (*Old English*).

Baptist *masc* a baptiser, purifier (*Greek*).

Baptista *fem* form of **Baptist**.

Baptiste *masc* a French form of **Baptist**.

Barbara, Barbra *fem* foreign, strange (*Greek*); diminutive forms are **Bab, Babs, Barbie**.

Barclay *masc* a surname, meaning birch wood, used as a first name (*Old English*); variant forms are **Berkeley, Berkley**.

Bard *masc* a variant form of **Baird**; a diminutive form of **Bardolph**.

Bardolph *masc* bright wolf (*Germanic*).

Barlow *masc* a surname, meaning barley hill or barley clearing, used as a first name (*Old English*).

Barnaby, Barnabas *masc* son of consolation and exhortation (*Hebrew*); a diminutive form is **Barney**.

Barnard *masc* a variant form of **Bernard**; a diminutive form is **Barney**.

Barnet, Barnett *masc* a surname, meaning land cleared by burning, used as a first name (*Old English*).

Barnum *masc* a surname, meaning homestead of a warrior, used as a first name (*Old English*).

Baron *masc* the lowest rank of the peerage used as a first name (*Old French*); a variant form is **Barron**.

Barratt, Barrett *masc* a surname, meaning commerce

or trouble or strife, used as a first name (*Old French*).

Barron *masc* a variant form of **Baron**.

Barry *masc* spear (*Irish Gaelic*).

Bart *masc* a diminutive form of **Bartholomew, Bartley, Barton, Bartram**.

Barthold *masc* variant form of **Berthold**.

Bartholomew *masc* a warlike son (*Hebrew*); diminutive forms are **Bart, Bat**.

Bartley *masc* a surname, meaning a birch wood or clearing, used as a first name (*Old English*); a diminutive form is **Bart**.

Barton *masc* the surname, meaning farm or farmyard, used as a first name (*Old English*); a diminutive form is **Bart**.

Bartram *masc* a variant form of **Bertram**.

Barzillal *masc* iron of the Lord; firm; true (*Hebrew*).

Basil *masc* kingly; royal (*Greek*).

Basile *masc* the French form of Basil.

Basilia *fem* form of **Basil**.

Basilio *masc* the Italian and Spanish form of **Basil**.

Bat *masc* a diminutive form of **Bartholomew**.

Bathilda *fem* battle commander (*Germanic*).

Bathilde *fem* the French form of **Bathilda**.

Bathsheba *fem* seventh daughter (*Hebrew*).

Batiste *masc* the French form of **Baptist**.

Battista *masc* the Italian form of **Baptist**.

Baudouin *masc* the French form of **Baldwin**.

Baudric *masc* a variant form of **Baldric**.

Bautista *masc* the Spanish form of **Baptist**.

Baxter *masc* a surname, meaning baker, used as a first name (*Old English*).

Bayley *masc* a variant form of **Bailey**.

Bea *fem* a diminutive form of **Beatrice, Beatrix**.

Beal, Beale, Beall *masc* a surname variant form of **Beau** used as a first name (*French*).

Beaman *masc* bee keeper (*Old English*); a variant form of **Beaumont** (*French*).

Beata *fem* blessed, divine one. Blessed and beloved of God (*Latin*); a diminutive form is **Bea**.

Beatrice, Beatrix *fem* happy (*Latin*); diminutive forms are **Bea, Beatie, Beaty, Bee, Trix, Trixie**.

Beau *masc* handsome (*French*); a diminutive form of **Beaufort, Beamont**.

Beaufort *masc* a surname, meaning beautiful stronghold, used as a first name (*French*); a diminutive form is **Beau**.

Beaumont *masc* a surname, meaning beautiful hill, used as a first name (*French*); a diminutive form is **Beau**.

Beavan, Beaven *masc* variant forms of **Bevan**.

Beckie, Becky *fem* diminutive forms of **Rebecca**.

Beda *fem* maid of war (*Old English*).

Bee *fem* a diminutive form of **Beatrice**.

Belinda *fem* a name used by Sir John Vanburgh in his play *The Provok'd Wife*, its origin is uncertain, possibly beautiful woman (*Italian*).

Bella, Belle *fem* beautiful (*French, Italian*); diminutive forms of **Annabel, Arabella, Isabella**.

Bellamy *masc* a surname, meaning handsome friend, used as a first name (*Old French*).

Ben *masc* a diminutive form of **Benedict, Benjamin**, also used independently.

Bena *fem* wise one (*Hebrew*).

Benedetto *masc* the Italian form of **Benedict**.

Benedict, Benedick *masc* blessed (*Latin*); *also* **Bennet**; diminutives are **Ben, Bennie, Benny**.

Benedicta *fem* form of **Benedict**; a contracted form is **Benita**; a diminutive form is **Dixie**.

Benedikt *masc* the German form of **Benedict**.

Beniamino *masc* the Italian form of **Benjamin**.

Benita *fem* form of **Benito**; a contracted form of **Benedicta**.

Benito *masc* a Spanish form of **Benedict**.

Benjamin *masc* son of the right hand (*Hebrew*); diminutive forms are **Ben, Benjie, Bennie, Benny**.

Benjie *masc* a diminutive form of **Benjamin**.

Bennet *masc* a variant form of **Benedict**.

Bennie, Benny *masc* a diminutive form of **Benedict, Benjamin**.

Benoît *masc* the French form of **Benedict**.

Benson *masc* a surname, meaning son of **Ben**, used as a first name.

Bentley *masc* a surname from a Yorkshire placename, meaning woodland clearing where bent-grass grows, used as a first name(*Old English*).

Beppe, Beppo *masc* a diminutive form of **Giuseppe**, occasionally used independently.

Berenice *fem* bringing victory (*Greek*); *also* **Bernice**.

Berkeley, Berkley *masc* variant forms of **Barclay**.

Bernadette *fem* form of **Bernard**.

Bernard *masc* strong or hardy bear (*Germanic*); *also* **Barnard**; diminutive forms are **Barney, Bernie**.

Bernardin *masc* a French form of **Bernard**.

Bernardino *masc* an Italian diminutive form of **Bernard**.

Bernardo *masc* a Spanish and Italian form of **Bernard**.

Bernhard, Bernhardt *masc* a German form of **Bernard**.

Bernice *fem* a variant form of **Berenice**.

Bernie *masc* a diminutive form of **Bernard**.

Bert *masc* diminutive forms of **Albert, Bertram, Egbert, Gilbert**, etc..

Berta *fem* a German, Italian and Spanish form of **Bertha**.

Bertha *fem* bright; beautiful; famous (*Germanic*); a diminutive form is **Bertie**.

Berthe *fem* the French form of **Bertha**.

Berthilda, Berthilde, Bertilda, Bertilde *fem* shining maid of war (*Old English*).

Berthold *masc* bright ruler (*Germanic*); variant forms are **Barthold, Bertold, Berthoud**; diminutive forms are **Bert, Bertie**.

Bertie *masc* diminutive forms of **Albert, Bertram, Egbert, Gilbert, Herbert**, etc; *fem* a diminutive form of **Bertha**.

Bertold, Berthoud *masc* variant forms of **Berthold**.

Bertram *masc* bright; fair; illustrious (*Germanic*); a variant form is **Bartram**; diminutive forms are **Bert, Bertie**.

Bertrand *masc* the French form of **Bertram**.

Beryl *fem* jewel (*Greek*), the name of the gemstone used as a first name.

Bess, Bessie *fem* diminutive forms of **Elizabeth**.

Beth *fem* a diminutive form of **Elizabeth, Bethany,** now used independently.

Bethan *fem* a Welsh diminutive form of **Elizabeth-Ann** also used independently.

Bethany *fem* a placename near Jerusalem, the home of Lazarus in the New Testament and meaning house of poverty, used as a first name (*Aramaic*).

Betsy, Bette, Bettina, Betty *fem* diminutive forms of **Elizabeth**.

Beulah *fem* land of rest (*Hebrew*).

Bevan *masc* a surname, meaning son of **Evan**, used as a first name (*Welsh*); variant forms are **Beavan, Beaven, Bevin**.

Beverley, Beverly *fem masc* a placename, meaning beaver stream, used as a first name (*Old English*); a diminutive form is **Bev**.

Bevin *masc* a surname, meaning drink wine, used as a first name; a variant form of Bevan.

Bevis *masc* bull (*French*).

Bianca *fem* the Italian form of **Blanch**, now also used independently as an English-language form.

Biddy *fem* a diminutive form of **Bridget**.

Bije *masc* a diminutive form of **Abijah**.

Bill *masc* a diminutive form of **William**.

Billie *masc* a diminutive form of **William**; *fem* a diminutive form of **Wilhelmina**.

Bina, Binah, Bine *fem* bee (*Hebrew*).

Bing *masc* a surname, meaning a hollow, used as a first name (*Germanic*).

Binnie *fem* a diminutive form of **Sabina**.

Birch *masc* a surname, from the birch tree, used as a first name (*Old English*); a variant form is **Birk**.

Birgit *fem* the Swedish form of **Bridget**; a diminutive form is **Britt**.

Birk *masc* a variant form of **Birch**.

Bishop *masc* a surname, meaning one who worked in a bishop's household, used as a first name (*Old English*).

Björn *masc* bear (*Old Norse*).

Black *masc* a surname, meaning dark-complexioned or dark-haired, used as a first name (*Old English*); a variant form is **Blake**.

Blair *masc* a placename and surname, meaning a plain, used as a first name (*Scottish Gaelic*).

Blaise *masc* sprouting forth (*French*).

Blake *masc* a variant form of Black; alternatively, pale or fair-complexioned (*Old English*).

Blanca *fem* the Spanish form of **Blanch**.

Blanche *fem* white (*Germanic*).

Bleddyn *masc* wolf (*Welsh*).

Bliss *masc*, *fem* a surname, meaning happiness or joy, used as a first name (*Old English*).

Blodwen *fem* white flower (*Welsh*).

Blossom *fem* like a flower (*Old English*).

Blyth, Blythe *masc*, *fem* a surname, meaning cheerful and gentle, used as a first name (*Old English*).

Boas, Boaz *masc* in the Lord's strength (*Hebrew*).

Bob, Bobbie, Bobby *masc* diminutive forms of **Robert**.

Bonar *masc* a surname, meaning gentle, kind, courteous, used as a first name (*French*); variant forms are **Bonnar, Bonner**.

Boniface *masc* a benefactor (*Latin*).

Bonita *fem* pretty (*Spanish*); good (*Latin*); a diminutive form is **Bonnie**.

Bonnar, Bonner *masc* variant forms of **Bonar**.

Bonnie *fem* pretty (*Scots English*); a diminutive form of **Bonita**.

Booth *masc* a surname, meaning hut or shed, used as a first name (*Old Norse*).

Boris *masc* small (*Russian*).

Botolf, Botolph *masc* herald wolf (*Old English*).

Bourn, Bourne *masc* variant forms of **Burn**.

Bowen *masc* a surname, meaning son of Owen, used as a first name (*Welsh*).

Bowie *masc* a surname, meaning yellow-haired, used as a first name (*Scots Gaelic*).

Boyce *masc* a surname, meaning a wood, used as a first name (*Old French*).

Boyd *masc* a surname, meaning light-haired, used as a first name (*Scots Gaelic*).

Boyne *masc* the name of an Irish river, meaning white cow, used as a first name (*Irish Gaelic*).

Brad *masc* a diminutive form of **Bradley**, now used independently.

Bradford *masc* a placename and surname, meaning place at the broad ford, used as a first name (*Old English*).

Bradley *masc* a surname, meaning broad clearing or broad wood, used as a first name (*Old English*); a diminutive form is **Brad**.

Brady *masc* a surname, of unknown meaning, used as a first name (*Irish Gaelic*).

Braham *masc* a surname, meaning house or meadow with broom bushes, used as a first name.

Bram *masc* a diminutive form of **Abram, Abraham**.

Bramwell *masc* a surname, meaning from the bramble spring, used as a first name (*Old English*).

Bran *masc* raven (*Gaelic*).

Brand *masc* firebrand (*Old English*).

Brandon *masc* a surname, meaning broom-covered hill, used as a first name (*Old English*); a variant form of **Brendan**.

Branwen *fem* raven-haired beauty (*Welsh*); a variant form of **Bronwen**.

Brenda *fem* a brand or sword (*Old Norse*).

Brendan *masc* prince (*Celtic*); a variant form is **Brandon**.

Brenna *fem* raven-haired beauty (*Irish Gaelic*).

Brent *masc* a surname, meaning a steep place, used as a first name (*Old English*).

Bret, Brett *masc* a Breton (*Old French*).

Brewster *masc* a surname, meaning brewer, used as a first name (*Old English*).

Brian *masc* strong (*Celtic*); a variant form is **Bryan**.

Brice *masc* a surname, of unknown meaning, used as a first name (*Celtic*); a variant form is **Bryce**.

Bridget *fem* shining bright (*Celtic*); a variant form is **Brigid**; diminutive forms are **Biddy, Bridie**.

Brigham *masc* a surname, meaning homestead by a bridge, used as a first name (*Old English*).

Brigid *fem* a variant form of **Bridget**.

Brigide *fem* a Spanish, Italian, and French form of **Bridget**.

Brigitte *fem* a French form of **Bridget**.

Briony *fem* a variant form of **Bryony**.

Britt *fem* a diminutive form of **Birgit**, now used independently.

Brittany *fem* the anglicized name of a French region, meaning land of the figured, or tattooed folk, used as a first name.

Brock *masc* a surname, meaning badger, used as a first name (*Old English*).

Broderic, Broderick *masc* a surname, meaning son of

Roderick, used as a first name (*Welsh*); brother (*Scots Gaelic*).

Brodie, Brody *masc* a surname, meaning ditch, used as a first name (*Scots Gaelic*).

Bron *masc* a diminutive form of **Auberon, Oberon**.

Bronwen *fem* white breast (*Welsh*); a variant form is **Branwen**.

Brook, Brooke *masc, fem* a surname, meaning stream, used as a first name; a variant form is **Brooks**.

Brooks *masc* a variant form of Brook.

Bruce *masc* a surname, originally from Normandy in France and of unknown meaning, used as a first name.

Brunella *fem* form of **Bruno**.

Brunhilda, Brunhilde *fem* warrior maid (*Germanic*).

Bruno *masc* brown (*Germanic*).

Bryan *masc* a variant form of **Brian**.

Bryce *masc* a variant form of **Brice**.

Bryn *masc* hill (*Welsh*).

Brynmor *fem* large hill (*Welsh*).

Bryony *fem* the name of a climbing plant used as a first name (*Greek*); a variant form is **Briony**.

Buck *masc* stag; he-goat; a lively young man (*Old English*).

Buckley *masc* a surname, meaning stag or he-goat meadow, used as a first name (*Old English*).

Budd, Buddy *masc* the informal term for a friend or brother used as a first name (*Old English*).

Buena *fem* good (*Spanish*).

Bunty *fem* a diminutive meaning lamb, now used as a first name (*English*).

Buona *fem* good (*Italian*).

Burchard *masc* a variant form of **Burkhard**.

Burdon *masc* a surname, meaning castle on a hill or valley with a cowshed, used as a first name (*Old English*).

Burford *masc* a surname, meaning ford by a castle, used as a first name (*Old English*).

Burgess *masc* a surname, meaning citizen or inhabitant of a borough, used as a first name (*Old French*).

Burk, Burke *masc* a surname, meaning fort or manor, used as a first name (*Old French*).

Burkhard *masc* strong as a castle (*Germanic*); a variant form is **Burchard**.

Burl *masc* cup bearer (*Old English*).

Burley *masc* Dweller in the castle by the meadow (*Old English*); a diminutive form is **Burleigh**.

Burn, Burne *masc* a surname, meaning brook or stream, used as a first name (*Old English*); variant forms are **Bourn, Bourne, Byrne**.

Burnett *masc* a surname, meaning brown-complexioned or brown-haired, used as a first name (*Old French*).

Burt *masc* a diminutive form of **Burton**, now used independently.

Burton *masc* a surname, meaning farmstead of a fortified placed, used as a first name (*Old English*); diminutive forms are **Burt**.

Buster *masc* an informal term of address for a boy or young man, now used as a first name (*English*).

Byrne *masc* a variant form of **Burn**.

Byron *masc* a surname, meaning at the cowsheds, used as a first name (*Old English*).

C

Caddie *fem* a diminutive form of **Carol, Carola, Carole, Caroline, Carolyn**.

Caddick, Caddock *masc* a surname, meaning decrepit or epileptic, used as a first name (*Old French*).

Cadell *masc* a surname, meaning battle spirit, used as a first name (*Welsh*).

Cadence *fem* rhythmic (*Latin*).

Cadenza *fem* the Italian form of **Cadence**.

Cadmus *masc* man from the east; in Greek mythology a Phoenician prince who founded Thebes with five warriors he had created (*Greek*).

Cadwalader *masc* battle arranger (*Welsh*).

Caesar *masc* long-haired; the Roman title of emperor used as a first name (*Latin*).

Cain *masc* possessed; the Biblical character who killed his brother Abel (*Hebrew*).

Cáit *fem* the Irish Gaelic form of **Kate**.

Caitlín, Caitrín *fem* Irish Gaelic forms of **Katherine**.

Cal *fem* a diminutive form of **Calandra, Calantha**.

Calandra *fem* lark(*Greek*); diminutive forms are **Cal, Callie, Cally**.

Calandre *fem* the French form of **Calandra**.

Calandria *fem* the Spanish form of **Calandra**.

Calantha *fem* beautiful blossom (*Greek*); diminutive forms are **Cal, Callie, Cally**.

Calanthe *fem* the French form of **Calantha**.

Calder *masc* a placename and surname, meaning hard or rapid water, used as a first name (*Celtic*).

Caldwell *masc* a surname, meaning cold spring or stream, used as a first name (*Old English*).

Caleb *masc* a dog (*Hebrew*); a diminutive form is **Cale**.

Caledonia *fem* the Roman name for Scotland used as a first name (*Latin*).

Caley *masc* thin, slender (*Irish Gaelic*); diminutive form of **Calum**.

Calhoun *masc* a surname, meaning from the forest, used as a first name (*Irish Gaelic*).

Calla *fem* beautiful (*Greek*).

Callie *fem* a diminutive form of **Calandra, Calantha**.

Calliope *fem* lovely voice; the muse of poetry (*Greek*).

Callisto *masc* most fair or good (*Greek*).

Callista *fem* form of **Callisto**.

Cally *fem* a diminutive form of **Calandra, Calantha**; *masc* diminutive form of **Calum**.

Calum, Callum *masc* the Scots Gaelic form of *Columba*, the Latin for dove; a diminutive form of **Malcolm**; diminutive forms are **Cally, Caley**.

Calumina *fem* form of **Calum**.

Calvert *masc* a surname, meaning calf herd, used as a first name (*Old English*).

Calvin *masc* little bald one (*Latin*).

Calvina *fem* form of **Calvin**.

Calvino *masc* and Italian and Spanish forms of **Calvin**.

Calypso *fem* concealer; in Greek mythology, the sea nymph who held Odysseus captive for seven years (*Greek*).a variant form is **Kalypso**.

Cameron *masc* a surname, meaning hook nose, used as a first name (*Scots Gaelic*).

Camila *fem* the Spanish form of **Camilla**.

Camilla *fem* attendant at a sacrifice (*Latin*).

Camille *masc, fem* the French form of **Camilla**.

Campbell *masc* a surname, meaning crooked mouth, used as a first name (*Scots Gaelic*).

Candie *fem* a diminutive form of **Candice, Candida**.

Candice, Candace *fem* meaning uncertain, possibly brilliantly white or pure and virtuous, the name of an Ethiopian queen (*Latin*); **Candie, Candy**.

Candida *fem* white (*Latin*); diminutive forms are **Candie, Candy**.

Candy *fem* a diminutive form of **Candice, Candida**; a name used in its own right, from candy, the American English word for a sweet.

Canice *masc* handsome or fair one (*Irish Gaelic*).

Canute *masc* knot (*Old Norse*), the name of a Danish king of England (1016–35); variant forms are **Cnut, Knut**.

Cara *fem* friend (*Irish Gaelic*); dear, darling (*Italian*); a variant form is **Carina**.

Caradoc, Caradog *masc* beloved (*Welsh*); a variant form is **Cradoc**.

Cardew *masc* a surname meaning black fort, used as a first name (*Welsh*).

Carey *masc* a surname, meaning castle dweller (*Welsh*) or son of the dark one (*Irish Gaelic*), used as a first name; a variant form of **Cary**.

Caridad *fem* the Spanish form of **Charity**.

Carina *fem* a variant form of **Cara**.

Carissa *fem* dear one (*Latin*).

Carl *masc* an anglicized German and Swedish form of **Charles**; a diminutive form of **Carlton, Carlin, Carlisle, Carlo, Carlos**.

Carla *fem* form of **Carl**; a variant form is **Carlin**; diminutive forms are **Carlie, Carley, Carly**.

Carleton *masc* a variant form of **Carlton**.

Carlie *fem* a diminutive form of **Carla, Carlin**.

Carlin *fem* a variant form of **Carla**; diminutive forms are **Carlie, Carley, Carly**.

Carlo *masc* the Italian form of **Charles**.

Carlos *masc* the Spanish form of **Charles**.

Carlotta *fem* the Italian form of **Charlotte**.

Carlton *masc* a placename and surname, meaning farm of the churls—a rank of peasant, used as a first name (*Old English*).variant forms are **Carleton, Charlton, Charleton**; a diminutive form is **Carl**.

Carly *fem* a diminutive form of **Carla, Carlin**, now used independently.

Carmel *fem* garden (*Hebrew*).

Carmela *fem* a Spanish and the Italian forms of **Carmel**.

Carmelita *fem* a Spanish diminutive form of **Carmel**.

Carmen *fem* a Spanish form of **Carmel**.

Carmichael *masc* a Scottish placename and surname, meaning fort of **Michael**, used as a first name (*Celtic*).

Carnation *fem* the name of a flower, meaning flesh colour, used as a first name (*Latin/French*).

Carol *masc* a shortened form of *Carolus*, the Latin form of **Charles**; *fem* a shortened form of **Caroline**; diminutive forms are **Caro, Carrie, Caddie**.

Carola *fem* a variant form of **Caroline**; diminutive forms are **Carrie, Caro, Caddie**.

Carole *fem* the French form of **Carol**; a contracted form of **Caroline**; diminutive forms are **Caro, Carrie, Caddie**.

Carolina *fem* the Italian and Spanish forms of **Caroline**.

Caroline, Carolyn *fem* form of *Carolus*, the Latin form of **Charles**; diminutive forms are **Caro, Carrie, Caddie**.

Carr *masc* a placename and surname, meaning overgrown marshy ground, used as a first name (*Old Norse*); variant forms are **Karr, Kerr**.

Carrie *fem* a diminutive form of **Carol, Carola, Carole, Caroline, Carolyn**.

Carrick *masc* a placename, meaning rock, used as a first name (*Gaelic*).

Carroll *masc* a surname, of uncertain meaning—possibly hacking, used as a first name (*Irish Gaelic*).

Carson *masc* a surname, of uncertain meaning but possibly marsh dweller (*Old English*), used as a first name.

Carter *masc* a surname, meaning a driver or maker of cars (*Old English*) or son of Arthur (*Scots Gaelic*), used as a first name.

Carver *masc* great rock (*Cornish Gaelic*); a surname, meaning sculptor, used as a first name (*Old English*).

Carwyn *masc* blessed love (*Welsh*).

Cary *masc* a surname, meaning pleasant stream, used as a first name (*Celtic*); a variant form is **Carey**.

Carys *fem* love (Welsh).

Casey *masc fem* an Irish surname, meaning vigilant, used as a first name; a placename, Cayce in Kentucky, where the hero Casey Jones was born, used as a first name; *fem* a variant form of **Cassie** used independently.

Cashel *masc* a placename, meaning circular stone fort, used as a first name (*Irish Gaelic*).

Casimir *masc* the English form of **Kasimir**.

Caspar, Casper *masc* the Dutch form of **Jasper**, now also used as an English-language form.

Cass *fem* a diminutive form of **Cassandra**; *masc* a diminutive form of **Cassidy, Cassius**.

Cassandra *fem* she who inflames with love (*Greek*); in Greek mythology, a princess whose prophecies of doom were not believed; diminutive forms are **Cass**, **Cassie**.

Cassidy *masc* a surname, meaning clever, used as a first name (*Irish Gaelic*); a diminutive form is **Cass**.

Cassie *fem* a diminutive form of **Cassandra**.

Cassian, Cassius *masc* a Roman family name, of uncertain meaning—possibly empty, used as a first name (*Latin*); a diminutive form is **Cass**.

Castor *masc* beaver (*Greek*).

Catalina *fem* the Spanish form of **Katherine**.

Caterina *fem* the Italian form of **Katherine**.

Cathal *masc* battle ruler (*Irish Gaelic*).

Catharina, Catharine, Catherina *fem* variant forms of **Catherine**.

Catherine *fem* the French form of **Katherine**, now used as an English-language form; diminutive forms are **Cath, Cathie, Cathy**.

Cato *masc* a Roman family name, meaning wise one, used as a first name (*Latin*).

Catrin *fem* the Welsh form of **Katherine**.

Catriona *fem* the Scots Gaelic form of **Katherine**.

Cavan *masc* a placename, meaning hollow with a grassy hill, used as a first name (*Irish Gaelic*); a variant form is **Kavan**.

Cecil *masc* dim-sighted (*Latin*).

Cecile *fem* the French form of **Cecily, Cecilia**.

Cécile *masc* the French form of **Cecil**.

Cecily, Cecilia *fem* forms of **Cecil**; diminutive forms are

Celia, Cis, Cissie, Cissy; a variant form is **Cicely**.

Cedric *masc* a name adapted by Sir Walter Scott for a character in *Ivanhoe* from the Saxon *Cerdic*, the first king of Wessex.

Ceinwen beautiful and blessed (*Welsh*).

Celandine *fem* the name of either of two unrelated flowering plants, meaning swallow, used as a first name (*Greek*).

Celeste, Celestine *fem* heavenly (*Latin*).

Celia *fem* heavenly (*Latin*); dimin of **Cecilia**.

Cemlyn *masc* a placename, meaning bending lake, used as a first name.

Cendrillon *fem* from the ashes, the fairytale heroine (*French*); the anglicized form is **Cinderella**.

Cephas *masc* a stone (*Aramaic*).

Ceri *masc* love (*Welsh*).

Cerian *fem* diminutive form of **Ceri**.

Cerys *fem* love (*Welsh*).

César *masc* the French form of **Caesar**.

Cesare *masc* the Italian form of **Caesar**.

Chad *masc* meaning uncertain—possibly warlike, bellicose (*Old English*).

Chaim *masc* a variant form of **Hyam**.

Chance *masc* the abstract noun for the quality of good fortune used as a first name (*Old French*); a variant form of **Chauncey**.

Chancellor *masc* a surname, meaning counsellor or secretary, used as a first name (*Old French*).

Chancey *masc* a variant form of **Chauncey**.

Chandler *masc* a surname, meaning maker or seller of candles, used as a first name (*Old French*).

Chandra *fem* moon brighter than the stars (*Sanskrit*).

Chanel *fem* the surname of the French couturier and perfumier, Coco Chanel, used as a first name.

Chapman *masc* a surname, meaning merchant, used as a first name (*Old English*).

Charis *fem* grace (*Greek*).

Charity *fem* the abstract noun for the quality of tolerance or genorosity used as a personal name (*Old French*).

Charlene *fem* a relatively modern diminutive form of **Charles**.

Charles *masc* strong; manly; noble-spirited (*Germanic*); a diminutive form is **Charlie**, **Charley**.

Charlie, Charley *masc, fem* diminutive forms of **Charles, Charlotte**.

Charlotte *fem* form of **Charles** (*Germanic*); diminutive forms are **Charlie, Charley, Lottie**.

Charlton, Charleton *masc* variant forms of **Carlton**.

Charmaine *fem* a diminutive form of the abstract noun for the quality of pleasing or attracting people used as a first name; a variant form of **Charmian**.

Charmian *fem* little delight (*Greek*); a modern variant form is **Charmaine**.

Chase *masc* a surname, meaning hunter, used as a first name (*Old French*).

Chauncey, Chaunce *masc* a surname, of uncertain meaning—possibly chancellor, used as a first name (Old French); variant forms are **Chance, Chancey**.

Chelsea *fem* a placename, meaning chalk landing place, used as a first name (*Old English*).

Cher, Chérie *fem* dear, darling (*French*).

Cherry *fem* the name of the fruit used as a first name; a form of **Chérie**; a variant form is **Cheryl**.

Cheryl *fem* a variant form of **Cherry**; a combining form of **Cherry** and **Beryl**; a variant form is **Sheryl**.

Chester *masc* a placename, meaning Roman fortified camp, used as a first name (*Old English*).

Chiara *fem* the Italian form of **Clara**.

Chilton *masc* a placename and surname, meaning children's farm, used as a first name (*Old English*).

Chiquita *fem* little one (*Spanish*).

Chloë, Chloe *fem* a green herb; a young shoot (*Greek*).

Chloris *fem* green (*Greek*).

Chris *masc fem* a diminutive form of **Christian, Christine, Christopher**.

Chrissie *fem* a diminutive form of **Christiana, Christine**.

Christabel *fem* a combination of **Christine** and **Bella** made by Samuel Taylor Coleridge for a poem of this name.

Christian *masc, fem* belonging to Christ; a believer in Christ (*Latin*); diminutive forms are **Chris, Christie, Christy**.

Christiana *fem* form of Christian; a variant form is
 Christina.

Christie *masc* a surname, meaning Christian, used as a
 first name; a diminutive form of **Christian, Christopher**; *fem* a diminutive form of **Christian, Christine**;
 a variant form is **Christy**.

Christina *fem* a variant form of **Christiana**.

Christine *fem* a French form of **Christina**, now used as
 an English-language form; diminutive forms are
 Chris, Chrissie, Christie, Christy, Teenie, Tina.

Christmas *masc* festival of Christ (*Old English*).

Christoph *masc* the German form of **Christopher**.

Christopher *masc* bearing Christ (*Greek*); diminutive
 forms are **Chris, Christie, Christy, Kester, Kit**.

Christy *masc fem* a variant form of **Christie**.

Chrystal *fem* a variant form of **Crystal**.

Churchill *masc* a placename and surname, meaning
 church on a hill, used as a first name (*Old English*).

Cian *masc* ancient (*Irish Gaelic*); anglicized forms are
 Kean, Keane.

Ciara *fem* form of **Ciarán**.

Ciarán *masc* small and black (*Irish Gaelic*); the anglicized form is **Kieran**.

Cicely *fem* a variant form of **Cecilia**.

Cilla *fem* a diminutive form of **Priscilla** (*French*).

Cinderella *fem* the anglicized form of **Cendrillon**, the
 fairytale heroine; diminutive forms are **Cindie, Cindy, Ella**.

Cindy *fem* a diminuntive form of **Cinderella, Cynthia, Lucinda**, now often used independently.

Cinzia *fem* the Italian form of **Cynthia**.

Claiborne *masc* a variant form of **Clayborne**; a diminutive form is **Clay**.

Claire *fem* the French form of **Clara**, now used widely as an English form.

Clara *fem* bright, illustrous (*Latin*); a variant form is **Clare**; a diminutive form is **Clarrie**.

Clarabel, Clarabella, Clarabelle *fem* a combination of **Clara** and **Bella** or **Belle**, meaning bright, shining beauty (*Latin/French*); a variant form is **Claribel**.

Clare *fem* a variant form of **Clara**; *fem, masc* a surname, meaning or bright, shining, used as a first name (*Latin*).

Clarence *masc* bright, shining (*Latin*); a diminutive form is **Clarrie**.

Claribel *fem* a variant form of **Clarabel**.

Clarice *fem* fame (*Latin*); a variant form of **Clara**; a variant form is **Clarissa**.

Clarinda *fem* a combination of **Clara** and **Belinda** or **Lucinda**.

Clarissa *fem* a variant form of **Clarice**.

Clark, Clarke *masc* a surname, meaning cleric, scholar or clerk, used as a first name (*Old French*).

Clarrie *fem* a diminutive form of **Clara**; *masc* a diminutive form of **Clarence**.

Claud *masc* the English form of **Claudius**.

Claude *masc* the French form of **Claud**; *fem* the French form of **Claudia**.

Claudia *fem* form of **Claud**.

Claudio *masc* the Italian and Spanish form of **Claud**.

Claudius *masc* lame (*Latin*); the Dutch and German forms of **Claud**.

Claus *masc* a variant form of **Klaus**.

Clay *masc* a surname, meaning a dweller in a place with clay soil, used as a first name (*Old English*); a diminutive form of **Claiborne, Clayborne, Clayton**.

Clayborne *masc* a surname, meaning a dweller in a place with clay soil by a brook, used as a first name (*Old English*); a variant form is Claiborne; a diminutive form is **Clay**.

Clayton *masc* a placename and surname, meaning place in or with good clay, used as a first name (*Old English*); a diminutive form is **Clay**.

Clem *fem* a diminutive form of **Clematis, Clemence, Clemency, Clementine, Clementina**; *masc* a diminutive form of **Clement**.

Clematis *fem* climbing plant (*Greek*), the name of a climbing plant with white, blue or purple flowers used as a first name; diminutive forms are **Clem, Clemmie**.

Clemency *fem* the abstract noun for the quality of tempering justice with mercy used as a first name (*Latin*); a variant form is **Clemence**; diminutive forms are **Clem, Clemmie**.

Clement *masc* mild-tempered, merciful (*Latin*); a diminutive form is **Clem**.

Clementine, Clementina *fem* forms of **Clement**; diminutive forms are **Clem, Clemmie**.

Cleo *fem* a short form of **Cleopatra**, used independently.

Cleopatra *fem* father's glory (*Greek*); a diminutive form is **Cleo**.

Cleveland *masc* a placename, meaning land of hills, used as a first name (*Old English*).

Cliantha *fem* glory flower (*Greek*); a diminutive form is **Clia**.

Cliff *masc* a diminutive form of **Clifford**, now used independently.

Clifford *masc* a surname, meaning ford at a cliff, used as a first name (*Old English*); a diminutive form is **Cliff**.

Clifton *masc* a placename, meaning place on a cliff, used as a first name (*Old English*).

Clint *masc* a diminutive form of Clinton, now used independently.

Clinton *masc* a placename and surname, meaning settlement on a hill, used as a first name; a diminutive form is **Clint**.

Clio *fem* glory (*Greek*).

Clive *masc* a surname, meaning at the cliff, used as a first name (*Old English*).

Clorinda *fem* a combination of **Chloris** and **Belinda** or **Lucinda**.

Clothilde, Clotilde *fem* famous fighting woman (*Germanic*).

Clover *fem* the name of a flowering plant used as a first name (*English*).

Clovis *masc* warrior (*Germanic*).

Clyde *masc* the name of a Scottish river, meaning cleansing one, used as a first name.

Cnut *masc* a variant form of **Canute**.

Cody *masc* a surname used as a first name.

Colby *masc* From the dark country (*Norse*).

Col *masc* a diminutive form of **Colman, Columba**.

Cole *masc* a diminutive form of **Coleman, Colman, Nicholas**; a surname, meaning swarthy or coal-black, used as a first name (*Old English*).

Coleman *masc* a surname, meaning swarthy man or servant of Nicholas, used as a surname (*Old English*).

Colette *fem* a diminutive form of **Nicole**, now used independently; a variant form is **Collette**.

Colin *masc* a diminutive form of **Nicholas**, long used independently.

Colleen *fem* the Irish word for a girl used as a first name.

Collette *fem* a variant form of **Colette**.

Collier, Collyer *masc* a surname, meaning charcoal seller or buirner, used as a first name (*Old English*); a variant form is **Colyer**.

Colm *masc* dove (*Irish Gaelic/Latin*)

Colman, Colmán *masc* keeper of doves (*Irish Gaelic/Latin*); diminutive forms are **Col, Cole**.

Colombe *masc, fem* the French form of Columba.

Columba *masc, fem* dove (*Latin*); a diminutive form is **Coly**.

Columbine *fem* little dove; the name of a flowering plant used as a first name (*Latin*).

Colyer *masc* a variant form of **Collier**.

Comfort *fem* the abstract noun for the state of well-being or bringer of solace used as a first name, in the Puritan tradition (*Latin/French*).

Comyn *masc* bent (*Irish Gaelic*).

Con *masc* a diminutive form of **Conan, Connall, Connor, Conrad**; *fem* a diminutive form of **Constance**, etc.

Conan, Cónán *masc* little hound (*Irish Gaelic*); a diminutive form is **Con**.

Concepción *fem* beginning, conception, a reference to the Immaculate Conception of the Virgin Mary (*Spanish*); diminutive forms are **Concha, Conchita**.

Concepta *fem* the Latin form of **Concetta**.

Concetta *fem* conceptive, a reference to the Virgin Mary and the Immaculate Conception (*Italian*).

Concha, Conchita *fem* diminutive forms of **Concepción**.

Conn *masc* chief (*Celtic*).

Connall *masc* courageous (*Irish and Scots Gaelic*).

Connor *masc* high desire or will (*Irish Gaelic*).

Conrad *masc* able counsel (*Germanic*).

Conrad *masc* able or brave counsellor (*Germanic*); a diminutive form is **Con**.

Conroy *masc* wise (*Gaelic*).

Consolata *fem* consoling, a reference to the Virgin Mary (*Italian*).

Consolation *fem* the abstract noun for the act of consoling or the state of solace used as a first name in the Puritan tradition.

Constance *fem* form of **Constant**; diminutive forms are **Con**, **Connie**; a variant form is **Constanta**.

Constant *masc* firm; faithful (*Latin*); a diminutive form is **Con**.

Constanta *fem* a variant form of **Constance**.

Constantine *masc* resolute; firm (*Latin*).

Constanza *fem* the Italian and Spanish forms of **Constance**.

Consuela *fem* consolation, a reference to the Virgin Mary (*Spanish*).

Consuelo *masc* consolation, a reference to the Virgin Mary (*Spanish*).

Conway *masc* a surname, of uncertain meaning—possibly yellow hound or head-smashing, used as a first name (*Irish Gaelic*); high or holy water (*Welsh*).

Cooper *masc* a surname, meaning barrel maker, used as a first name (*Old English*); a diminutive form is **Coop**.

Cora *fem* maiden (*Greek*).

Corabella, **Corabelle** *fem* beautiful maiden, a combination of **Cora** and **Bella**.

Coral *fem* the name of the pink marine jewel material used as a first name.

Coralie *fem* the French form of **Coral**.

Corazón *fem* (sacred) heart (Spanish).

Corbet, Corbett *masc* a surname, meaning raven, black-haired or raucousness, used as a first name (*Old French*).

Corcoran *masc* a surname, meaning red- or purple-faced, used as a first name (*Irish Gaelic*).

Cordelia *fem* warm-hearted (*Latin*).

Corey *masc* a surname, meaning god peace, used as a first name (*Irish Gaelic*).

Corinna, Corinne *fem* variant forms of **Cora**.

Cormac, Cormack, Cormick *masc* charioteer (*Irish Gaelic*).

Cornelia *fem* form of **Cornelius**.

Cornelius *masc* origin uncertain, possibly horn-like, a Roman family name; a variant form is **Cornell**.

Cornell masc a surname, meaning Cornwall or a hill where corn is sold, used as a first name; a variant form of **Cornelius**.

Corona *fem* crown (*Latin*).

Corrado *masc* the Italian form of **Conrad**.

Corwin *masc* friend of the heart (*Old French*)

Cosima *fem* form of **Cosmo**.

Cosimo *masc* an Italian form of **Cosmo**.

Cosmo *masc* order, beauty (*Greek*).

Costanza *fem* an Italian form of **Constance**.

Courtney *masc, fem* a surname, meaning short nose, used as a first name (*Old French*).

Cradoc *masc* a variant form of **Caradoc**.

Craig *masc* a surname meaning crag, used as a first name (*Scots Gaelic*).

Cranley *masc* a surname, meaning crane clearing, spring or meadow, used as a first name (*Old English*).

Crawford *masc* a placename and surname, meaning ford of the crows, used as a first name (*Old English*).

Creighton *masc* a surname, meaning rock or cliff place (*Old Welsh*, *Old English*) or border settlement (*Scots Gaelic*), used as a first name (*Old English*).

Crépin *masc* the French form of **Crispin**.

Cressida *fem* gold (*Greek*); a contracted form is **Cressa**.

Crispin, Crispian *masc* having curly hair (*Latin*).

Crispus *masc* the German form of **Crispin**.

Cristal *fem* a variant form of **Crystal**.

Cristiano *masc* the Italian and Spanish form of **Christian**.

Cristina *fem* the Italian, Portuguese and Spanish form of **Christina**.

Cristóbal *masc* the Spanish form of **Christopher**.

Cristoforo *masc* the Italian form of **Christopher**.

Cromwell *masc* a placename and surname, meaning winding spring, used as a first name.

Crosbie, Crosby *masc* a placename and surname, meaning farm or village with crosses, used as a first name (*Old Norse*).

Crystal *fem* the name of a very clear brilliant glass used as a first name; variant forms are **Cristal, Chrystal**.

Cullan, Cullen *masc* a surname, meaning Cologne, used as a first name (*Old French*); a placename, meaning at the back of the river, used as a first name (*Scots Gaelic*).

Culley *masc* a surname, meaning woodland, used as a first name (*Scots Gaelic*).

Curran *masc* a surname, of uncertain meaning—possibly resolute hero, used as a first name (*Irish Gaelic*).

Curt *masc* a variant form of **Kurt**; a diminutive form of **Curtis**.

Curtis *masc* a surname, meaning courteous, educated, used as a first name (*Old French*); a diminutive form is **Curt**.

Cuthbert *masc* noted splendour (*Old English*).

Cy *masc* a diminutive form of **Cyrus**.

Cynthia *fem* belonging to Mount Cynthus (*Greek*); diminutive forms are **Cindie, Cindy**.

Cyprian *masc* from Cyprus, the Mediterranean island (*Greek*).

Cyrano *masc* from Cyrene, an ancient city of North Africa (*Greek*).

Cyrene, Cyrena *fem* from Cyrene, an ancient city of North Africa; in Greek mythology, a water nymph loved by Apollo (*Greek*); a variant form is **Kyrena**.

Cyril *masc* lordly (*Greek*).

Cyrill *masc* the German form of **Cyril**.

Cyrille *masc* the French form of Cyril; *fem* form of Cyril (*French*).

Cyrillus

Cyrillus *masc* the Danish, Dutch and Swedish forms of Cyril.

Cyrus *masc* the sun (*Persian*); a diminutive form is **Cy**.

Cytherea *fem* from Cythera, an island off the southern coast of the Peloponnese, in Greek mythology, home of a cult of Aphrodite (*Greek*).

Cythereia *fem* from Cytherea, in Greek mythology, an alternative name for Aphrodite.

D

Daffodil *fem* the name of the spring plant that yields bright yellow flowers used as a first name (*Dutch/Latin*); a diminutive form is **Daffy**.

Dafydd *masc* a Welsh form of **David**.

Dag *masc* day (*Norse*).

Dagan *masc* earth, the name of an earth god of the Assyrians and Babylonians (*Semitic*).

Dagmar *fem* bright day (*Norse*).

Dahlia *fem* the name of the plant with brightly coloured flowers, named after the Swedish botanist Anders Dahl (dale), used as a first name.

Dai *masc* a Welsh diminutive form of David, formerly a name in its own right, meaning shining.

Daisy *fem* the name of the plant; the day's eye (*Old English*).

Dale *masc fem* a surname, meaning valley, used as a first name (*Old English*).

Daley *masc, fem* a surname, meaning assembly, used as a first name (*Irish Gaelic*); a variant form is **Daly**.

Dalilah, Dalila *fem* variant forms of **Delilah**.

Dallas *masc* a surname, meaning meadow resting place

(*Scots Gaelic*) or dale house (*Old English*), used as a first name.

Dalton *masc* a surname, meaning dale farm, used as a first name (*Old English*).

Daly *masc, fem* a variant of **Daley**.

Dalziel *masc* a placename and surname, meaning field of the sungleam, used as a first name (*Scots Gaelic*).

Damian *masc* the French form of **Damon**.

Damiano *masc* the Italian form of **Damon**.

Damien *masc* taming (*Greek*).

Damon *masc* conqueror (*Greek*).

Dan *masc* a diminutive form of **Danby, Daniel**.

Dana *masc, fem* a surname, of uncertain meaning—possibly Danish, used as a first name (*Old English*); *fem* form of **Dan, Daniel**.

Danaë *fem* in Greek mythology, the mother of Perseus by Zeus, who came to her as shower of gold while she was in prison; diminutive forms are **Dannie, Danny**.

Danby *masc* a placename and surname, meaning Danes' settlement, used as a first name (*Old Norse*); a diminutive form is **Dan**.

Dandie *masc* a Scottish diminutive form of **Andrew**.

Dane *masc* a surname, meaning valley, used as a first name (*Old English*).

Daniel *masc* a divine judge (*Hebrew*); diminutive forms are **Dan, Dannie, Danny**.

Danielle *fem* form of **Daniel**; *masc* the Italian form of **Daniel**.

Dannie, Danny *masc* diminutives of **Danby, Daniel**; *fem* diminutives of **Danaë, Danielle**.

Dante *masc* steadfast (*Latin/Italian*).

Daphne *fem* laurel (*Greek*).

Dara *fem* charity (*Hebrew*); *masc* oak (*Irish Gaelic*).

Darby *masc* a variant form of Derby, a surname meaning a village where deer are seen, used as a surname (*Old Norse*); a diminutive form of **Dermot, Diarmid** (*Irish Gaelic*).

Darcie *fem* form of **Darcy**.

Darcy, D'Arcy *masc* a surname, meaning fortress, used as a first name (*Old French*).

Darell *masc* a variant form of **Darrell**.

Daria *fem* form of **Darius**.

Darien *masc* a South American placename used as a first name.

Dario *masc* the Italian form of **Darius**.

Darius *masc* preserver (*Persian*).

Darlene, Darleen *fem* the endearment 'darling' combined with a suffix to form a first name (*Old English*).

Darnell *masc* a surname, meaning hidden nook, used as a first name (*Old English*).

Darrell, Darrel *masc* from a surname, meaning from Airelle in Normandy, used as a first name; variant forms are **Darell, Darryl, Daryl**.

Darrelle *fem* form of Darrell (*French*).

Darren, Darin *masc* a surname, of unknown origin, used as a first name.

Darryl a variant form of **Darrell**, also used as a girl's name.

Darton *masc* a surname, meaning deer enclosure or forest, used as a first name (*Old English*).

Daryl a variant form of **Darrell**, also used as a girl's name.

David *masc* beloved (*Hebrew*); diminutive forms are **Dave, Davie, Davy**.

Davidde *masc* the Italian form of David.

Davide *masc* the French form of **David**.

Davie *masc* a diminutive form of **David**.

Davin *masc* a variant form of **Devin**.

Davina *fem* form of **David**.

Davis *masc* David's son (*Old English*).

Davy *masc* a diminutive form of **David**.

Dawn *fem* the name of the first part of the day used as a personal name (*English*).

Dean *masc* a surname, meaning one who lives in a valley (*Old English*) or serving as a dean (*Old French*), used as a first name; the anglicized form of **Dino**.

Deana, Deane *fem* forms of Dean; variant forms are **Dena, Dene**.

Deanna *fem* a variant form of **Diana**.

Dearborn *masc* a surname, meaning deer brook, used as a first name (*Old English*).

Deborah, Debra *fem* a bee (*Hebrew*); diminutive forms are **Deb, Debbie, Debby**.

Decima *fem* form of Decimus.

Decimus *masc* tenth (*Latin*).

Declan *masc* the name, of unknown meaning, of a 5th-century Irish saint (*Irish Gaelic*).

Dedrick *masc* people's ruler (*Germanic*).

Dee *fem* a diminutive form of names beginning with D.

Deinol *masc* charming (*Welsh*).

Deirdre *fem* meaning uncertain, possibly sorrowful (*Irish Gaelic*).

Delfine *fem* a variant form of **Delphine**.

Delia *fem* woman of Delos (*Greek*).

Delicia *fem* great delight (*Latin*).

Delight *fem* the abstract noun for great pleasure, satisfaction or joy used as a first name (*Old French*).

Delilah, Delila *fem* meaning uncertain, possibly delicate (*Hebrew*); a variant forms are **Dalila, Dalilah**; a diminutive form is **Lila**.

Dell *masc* a surname, meaning one who lives in a hollow, used as a first name; a diminutive form of **Delmar**, etc.

Delma *fem* form of **Delmar**; a diminutive form of **Fidelma**.

Delmar *masc* of the sea (*Latin*).

Delores *fem* a variant form of **Dolores**.

Delphine *fem* woman of Delphi (*Latin*); a variant form is **Delfine**.

Delwyn, Delwin *masc* neat and blessed (*Welsh*).

Delyth *fem* pretty (*Welsh*).

Demetria *fem* form of **Demeter**.

Demetre *masc* the French form of **Demetrius**.

Demetrio *masc* the Italian form of **Demetrius**.

Demetrius *masc* belonging to Demeter, Greek goddess of corn or the earth; sprung from the earth (*Greek*).

Dempsey *masc* a surname, meaning proud descendant, used as a first name (*Gaelic*).

Dempster *masc* a surname, meaning judge, used as a first name, formerly a feminine one (*Old English*).

Den *masc* diminutive form of **Denis, Dennis, Denison, Denley, Denman, Dennison, Denton, Denver, Denzel, Denzell, Denzil**.

Dena, Dene *fem* variant forms of **Deana**.

Denby *masc* a surname, meaning Danish settlement, used as a first name (*Norse*).

Denice *fem* a variant form of **Denise**.

Denis, Dennis *masc* belonging to Dionysus, the god of wine (*Greek*).

Denise *fem* form of **Denis**; a variant form is **Denice**.

Denison *masc* a variant form of **Dennison**.

Denley *masc* a surname, meaning wood or clearing in a valley, used as a first name (*Old English*).

Denman *masc* a surname, meaning dweller in a valley, used as a first name (*Old English*).

Dennison *masc* son of Dennis (*Old English*); variant forms are **Denison, Tennison, Tennyson**.

Denton *masc* a surname, meaning valley place, used as a first name (*Old English*).

Denver *masc* a surname, meaning Danes' crossing, used

as a first name (*Old English*).

Denzel, Denzell, Denzil *masc* a surname, meaning stronghold, used as a first name (*Celtic*).

Deon *masc* a variant form of **Dion**.

Derek, *masc* an English form of **Theoderic**; variant forms are **Derrick, Derrik**; a diminutive form is **Derry**.

Dermot *masc* the anglicized form of **Diarmaid**; a diminutive form is **Derry**.

Derrick, Derrik *masc* variant forms of **Derek**; a diminutive form is **Derry**.

Derry *masc* the anglicized form of a placename, meaning oak wood, used as a first name (*Irish Gaelic*); a diminutive form of **Derek, Derrick, Derrik, Dermot**.

Derwent *masc* a placename and surname, meaning river that flows through oak woods, used as a first name (*Old English*).

Desdemona *fem* ill-fated (*Greek*), the name given by Shakespeare to the wife of Othello.

Desirée *fem* longed for (*French*).

Desmond *masc* from south Munster (*Irish Gaelic*).

Deverell, Deverill *masc* a surname, meaning fertile river bank, used as a first name (*Celtic*).

Devin, Devinn *masc* a surname, meaning poet, used as a first name (*Irish Gaelic*); a variant form is **Davin**.

Devlin *masc* fiercely brave (*Irish Gaelic*).

Devon *masc* the name of the English county, meaning deep ones, used as a first name (*Celtic*)

Devona *fem* form of **Devon**.

77

Dewey *masc* a Celtic form of **David**.

Dewi *masc* a Welsh form of **David**.

De Witt *masc* fair-haired (*Flemish*).

Dexter *masc* a surname, meaning (woman) dyer, used as a first name (*Old English*).

Di *fem* a diminutive form of **Diana, Diane, Dianne, Dina, Dinah**.

Diamond *masc* the name of the gem, meaning the hardest iron or steel, used as a first name (*Latin*).

Diana *fem* goddess (*Latin*); a diminutive form is **Di**.

Diane, Dianne *fem* French forms of **Diana**.

Diarmaid *masc* free of envy (*Irish Gaelic*); a variant form is **Diarmuid**; the anglized form is **Dermot**.

Diarmid *masc* the Scottish Gaelic form of **Diarmaid**.

Diarmuid *masc* a variant form of **Diarmaid**.

Dick, Dickie, Dickon *masc* diminutive forms of **Richard**.

Dickson *masc* a surname, meaning son of Richard, used as a first name (*Old English*); a variant form is **Dixon**.

Dicky *masc* a diminutive form of **Richard**.

Dido *fem* teacher (*Greek*), in Greek mythology a princess from Tyre who founded Carthage and became its queen.

Diego *masc* a Spanish form of **James**.

Dietrich *masc* the German form of **Derek**; a diminutive form is **Till**.

Digby *masc* a surname, meaning settlement at a ditch, used as a first name (*Old Norse*).

Dillon *masc* a surname of uncertain meaning, possibly destroyer, used as a first name (*Germanic/Irish Gaelic*).

Dilys *fem* sure, genuine (*Welsh*); a diminutive form is **Dilly**.

Dina *fem* form of **Dino**; a variant form of **Dinah**.

Dinah *fem* judged (*Hebrew*); a variant form is **Dina**; a diminutive form is **Di**.

Dino *masc* a diminutive ending, indicating little, now used independently (*Italian*).

Dion *masc* a shortened form of Dionysus, the god of wine (*Greek*); a variant form is **Deon**.

Dione, Dionne *fem* daughter of heaven and earth (*Greek*), in Greek mythology the earliest consort of Zeus and mother of Aphrodite.

Dirk *masc* the Dutch form of **Derek**; a diminutive form of **Theodoric**.

Dixie *fem* a diminutive form of Benedicta.

Dixon *masc* a variant form of **Dickson**.

Dodie, Dodo *fem* diminutive forms of **Dorothy**.

Dolan *masc* a variant form of **Doolan**.

Dolina *fem* a Scottish diminutive form of **Donalda**.

Dolly *fem* a diminutive form of **Dorothy**.

Dolores *fem* sorrows (*Spanish*); a variant form is **Delores**; diminutive forms are **Lola**, **Lolita**.

Dolph *masc* a diminutive form of **Adolph**.

Domenico *masc* the Italian form of **Dominic**.

Domingo *masc* the Spanish form of **Dominic**.

Dominic, Dominick *masc* lord (*Latin*); a diminutive form is **Dom**.

Dominique *masc* the French form of **Dominic**, now used in English as a girl's name.

Don *masc* a diminutive form of **Donal, Donald, Donall**.

Dónal *masc* an Irish Gaelic form of **Donald**.

Donal *masc* anglicized forms of **Dónal**; a variant form is **Donall**; diminutive forms are **Don, Donnie, Donny**.

Donald *masc* proud chief (*Scots Gaelic*); diminutive forms are **Don, Donnie, Donny**.

Donalda *fem* form. of **Donald**.

Donall *masc* a variant form of **Donal**.

Donata *fem* form of **Donato**.

Donato *masc* gift of God (*Latin*).

Donna *fem* lady (*Italian*).

Donnie, Donny *masc* diminutive forms of **Donal, Donald, Donall**.

Doolan *masc* a surname, meaning black defiance, used as a first name (*Irish Gaelic*); a variant form is **Dolan**.

Dora *fem* a diminutive form of **Dorothea, Theodora**, etc, now used independently; diminutive forms are **Dorrie, Dorry**.

Doran *masc* a surname, meaning stranger or exile, used as a first name (*Irish Gaelic*).

Dorcas *fem* a gazelle (*Greek*).

Doreen *fem* an Irish variant form of **Dora**.

Dorian *masc* Dorian man, one of a Hellenic people who

invaded Greece in the 2nd century BC (*Greek*); its use as a first name was probably invented by Oscar Wilde for his novel, *The Picture of Dorian Gray*.

Dorinda *fem* lovely gift (*Greek*); diminutive forms are **Dorrie, Dorry**.

Doris *fem* Dorian woman, one of a Hellenic people who invaded Greece in the 2nd century BC (*Greek*); diminutive forms are **Dorrie, Dorry**.

Dorothea *fem* a German form of **Dorothea**; a diminutive form is **Thea**.

Dorothée *fem* a French form of **Dorothea**.

Dorothy *fem* the gift of God (*Greek*); diminutive forms are **Dodie, Dodo, Dolly, Dot**.

Dorrie, Dorry *fem* diminutive forms of **Dora, Dorinda, Doris**.

Dorward *masc* a variant form of **Durward**.

Dougal, Dougall *masc* black stranger (*Gaelic*); variant forms are **Dugal, Dugald**; diminutive forms are **Doug, Dougie, Duggie**.

Douglas *masc fem* a placename, meaning black water, used as a first name (*Scots Gaelic*); diminutive forms are **Doug, Dougie, Duggie**.

Dow *masc* a surname, meaning black or black-haired, used as a first name (*Scots Gaelic*).

Doyle *masc* an Irish Gaelic form of **Dougal**.

D'Oyley *masc* a surname, meaning from Ouilly—rich land, used as a first name (*Old French*).

Drake *masc* a surname, meaning dragon or standard bearer, used as a first name (*Old English*).

Drew *masc* a diminutive form of **Andrew**; a surname, meaning ghost (*Germanic*) or lover (*Old French*) used as a first name.

Driscoll, Driscol *masc* a surname, meaning interpreter, used as a first name (*Irish Gaelic*).

Druce *masc* a surname, meaning from Eure or Rieux in France (*Old French*), or sturdy lover, used as a first name (*Celtic*).

Drummond *masc* a surname, meaning ridge, used as a first name.

Drury *masc* a surname, meaning dear one, used as a first name (*Old French*).

Drusilla *fem* with dewy eyes (*Latin*).

Dryden *masc* a surname, meaning dry valley, used as a first name (*Old English*).

Duane *masc* dark (*Irish Gaelic*); variant forms are **Dwane, Dwayne**.

Dudley *masc* a placename, meaning Dudda's clearing, used as a first name (*Old English*).

Duff *masc* a surname, meaning black- or dark-complexioned, used as a first name (*Scots Gaelic*).

Dugal, Dugald *masc* variant forms of **Dougal**; a diminutive form is **Duggie**.

Duggie *masc* a diminutive form of **Dougal, Dougald, Douglas, Dugal, Dugald**.

Duke *masc* the title of an English aristocrat used as a first name; a diminutive form of **Marmaduke**.

Dulcie *fem* sweet (*Latin*).

Duncan *masc* brown chief (*Gaelic*); a diminutive form is **Dunc**.

Dunlop *masc* a surname, meaning muddy hill, used as a first name (*Scots Gaelic*).

Dunn, Dunne *masc* a surname, meaning dark-skinned, used as a first name (*Old English*).

Dunstan *masc* brown hill stone (*Old English*).

Durand, Durant *masc* a surname, meaning enduring or obstinate, used as a first name (*Old French*).

Durward *masc* a surname, meaning doorkeeper or gate-keeper, used as a first name (*Old English*); a variant form is **Dorward**.

Durwin *masc* Dear friend *Old English*); a diminutive form is **Durwyn**.

Dustin *masc* a surname, of uncertain meaning—possibly of Dionysus, used as a first name.

Dwane, Dwayne *masc* variant forms of **Duane**.

Dwight *masc* a surname, meaning Thor's stone, used as a first name (*Old Norse*).

Dyan *fem* a variant form of **Diane**.

Dyfan *masc* ruler (*Welsh*).

Dylan *masc* sea (*Welsh*).

Dymphna *fem* little fawn (*Irish Gaelic*).

E

Eachan, Eachann, Eacheann *masc* horse (*Scots Gaelic*).

Eamon, Eamonn *masc* an Irish Gaelic form of **Edmund**.

Éanna bird (*Irish Gaelic*); an anglicized form is **Enda**.

Earl, Earle *masc* an English title, meaning nobleman, used as a first name (*Old English*); a variant form is **Erle**.

Earlene, Earline *fem* form of **Earl**; variant forms are **Erlene, Erline**; diminutive forms are **Earlie, Earley**.

Eartha *fem* of the earth (*Old English*); a variant form is **Ertha**.

Easter *fem* the name of the Christian festival, meaning used as a first name.

Eaton *masc* a surname, meaning river or island farm, used as a first name (*Old English*).

Ebba *fem* wild boar (*Germanic*); an Old English form of **Eve**.

Eben *masc* stone (*Hebrew*); a diminutive form is **Eb**.

Ebenezer *masc* the stone of help (*Hebrew*); diminutive forms are **Eb, Eben**.

Eberhard, Ebert *masc* German forms of **Everard**.

Ebony *fem* the name of the dark hard wood used as a first name.

Echo *fem* the name for the physical phenomenon of the reflection of sound or orther radiation used as a first name; in Greek mythology it is the name of the nymph who pined away for love of Narcissus.

Ed *masc* a diminutive form of **Edbert, Edgar, Edmund, Edward, Edwin.**

Eda *fem* prosperity, happiness (*Old English*).

Edan *masc* a Scottish form of **Aidan.**

Edana *fem* form of **Edan.**

Edbert *masc* prosperous; bright (*Old English*).

Eddie, Eddy *masc* diminutive forms of **Edbert, Edgar, Edmund, Edward, Edwin**.

Edel *masc* noble (*Germanic*).

Edelmar *masc* noble, famous (*Old English*).

Eden *masc* place of pleasure (*Hebrew*); a surname, meaning blessed helmet, used as a first name.

Edgar *masc* giver of happiness (*Old English*); diminutive forms are **Ed, Eddie, Eddy, Ned, Neddie, Neddy**.

Edie *fem* a diminutive form of **Edina, Edith, Edwina.**

Edina *fem* a Scottish variant form of **Edwina.**

Edith *fem* happiness; rich gift (*Old English*); variant forms are **Edyth, Edythe**; diminutive forms are **Edie, Edy**.

Edlyn *fem* noble maid (*Old English*).

Edmond *masc* the French form of **Edmund.**

Edmonda *fem* form of Edmund (*Old English*).

Edmund *masc* defender of happiness (*Old English*).

Edna *fem* pleasure (*Hebrew*).

Edoardo *masc* an Italian form of **Edward**.

Édouard *masc* the French form of **Edward**.

Edrea *fem* form of **Edric**.

Edric *masc* wealthy ruler (*Old English*).

Edryd *masc* restoration (*Welsh*).

Edsel *masc* noble (*Germanic*).

Eduardo *masc* the Italian and Spanish form of **Edward**.

Edwald *masc* prosperous ruler (*Old English*).

Edward *masc* guardian of happiness (*Old English*); diminutive forms are **Ed, Eddie, Eddy, Ned, Ted, Teddy**.

Edwardina *fem* form of **Edward**.

Edwige *fem* the French form of **Hedwig**.

Edwin *masc* gainer of happiness (*Old English*).

Edwina *fem* form of **Edwin**; a variant form is **Edina**.

Edy *fem* a diminutive form of **Edith**.

Edyth, Edythe *fem* variant forms of **Edith**.

Effie *fem* a diminutive form of **Euphemia**.

Egan *masc* a surname, meaning son of Hugh, used as a first name (*Irish Gaelic*).

Egbert *masc* the sword's brightness; famous with the sword (*Germanic*).

Egberta *fem* form of Egbert (*Old English*).

Egidio *masc* the Italian and Spanish form of **Giles**.

Eglantine *fem* an alternative name for the wild rose,

meaning sharp, keen, used as a first name (*Old French*).

Ehren *masc* Honourable one (*Germanic*).

Eileen *fem* the Irish form of **Helen**; a variant form is **Aileen**.

Eilidh *fem* a Scots Gaelic form of **Helen**.

Eilir *masc* butterfly (*Welsh*).

Einar *masc* single warrior (*Old Norse*).

Eira *fem* snow (*Welsh*).

Eirlys *fem* snowdrop (*Welsh*).

Eithne *fem* kernel (*Irish Gaelic*); anglicized forms are **Ena, Ethna**.

Elaine *fem* a French form of **Helen**.

Elder *masc* a surname, meaning senior, elder, used as a first name (*Old English*).

Eldon *masc* a surname, meaning Ella's hill, used as a first name (*Old English*).

Eldora *fem* a shortened form of El Dorado, meaning the land of gold, used as a first name (*Spanish*).

Eldred *masc* terrible (*Old English*).

Eldrida *fem* form.of **Eldrid**.

Eldrid, Eldridge *masc* wise adviser (*Old English*).

Eleanor, Eleanore *fem* variant forms of **Helen**; a variant form is **Elinor**; diminutive forms are **Ella, Nell, Nora**.

Eleanora *fem* the Italian form of **Eleanor**.

Eleazer *masc* a variant form of **Eliezer**..

Electra *fem* brilliant (*Greek*).

Elen *fem* angel, nymph (*Welsh*).

Elena *fem* the Italian and Spanish form of **Helen**.

Eleonora *fem* the Italian form of **Eleanor**.

Eleonore *fem* the German form of **Eleanor**.

Eléonore *fem* a French form of **Leonora**.

Elfed *masc* autumn (*Welsh*).

Elfleda *fem* noble beauty (*Old English*).

Elfreda *fem* elf strength (*Old English*).

Elga *fem* holy (*Old Norse*); a variant form of **Olga**.

Elgan *masc* bright circle (*Welsh*).

Eli *masc* a diminutive form of **Elias, Elijah, Eliezer**; a variant form is **Ely**.

Elias *masc* a variant form of **Elijah**; a diminutive form is **Eli**.

Eliezer *masc* my God is help (*Hebrew*); a variant form is **Eleazar**.

Elihu *masc* God the Lord (*Hebrew*).

Elijah *masc* Jehovah is my lord (*Hebrew*); a diminutive form is **Lije**.

Elin *fem* a Welsh diminutive form of **Elinor**; a Welsh variant form of **Helen**.

Elinor *fem* a variant form of **Eleanor**.

Eliot *masc* a variant form of **Elliot**.

Elis *masc* a Welsh form of **Elias**.

Elisa *fem* an Italian diminutive form of **Elisabetta**.

Elisabeth *fem* a French and German form of **Elizabeth**.

Elisabetta *fem* an Italian form of **Elizabeth**.

Élise *fem* a French diminutive form of **Elisabeth**.

Elisha *masc* God my salvation (*Hebrew*).

Elizabeth *fem* worshiper of God; consecrated to God (*Hebrew*); diminutive forms are **Bess, Bet, Beth, Betsy, Betty, Eliza, Elsa, Elsie, Libby, Lisa, Liza, Lisbeth, Liz.**

Ella *fem* a diminutive form of **Cinderella, Eleanor, Isabella.**

Ellen *fem* a variant form of **Helen.**

Ellice *fem* form of **Elias, Ellis.**

Ellie *fem* a diminutive form of **Alice.**

Elliot, Elliot *masc* a surname, from a French diminutive form of Elias, used as a first name.

Ellis *masc* a surname, a Middle English form of **Elias,** used as a first name.

Ellison *masc* a surname, meaning son of Elias, used as a first name (*Old English*).

Elma *fem* a diminutive form of **Wilhelmina;** a contracted form of **Elizabeth Mary.**

Elmer *masc* noble; excellent (*Old English*).

Elmo *masc* amiable (*Greek*).

Elmore *masc* a surname, meaning river bank with elms, used as a first name (*Old English*).

Éloise, Eloisa *fem* sound, whole (*Germanic*); a variant form is **Héloïse.**

Elroy *masc* a variant form of **Leroy.**

Elsa *fem* a diminutive form of **Alison, Alice, Elizabeth.**

Elsie *fem* a diminutive form of **Alice, Alison, Elizabeth, Elspeth.**

Elspeth, Elspet *fem* Scottish forms of **Elizabeth**; diminutive forms are **Elsie, Elspie**.

Elton *masc* a surname, meaning settlement of Ella, used as a first name (*Old English*).

Eluned *fem* idol (*Welsh*).

Elva *fem* friend of the elf (*Old English*); a variant form is **Elvina**.

Elvey *masc* a surname, meaning elf gift, used as a first name (*Old English*); a variant form is **Elvy**.

Elvin *masc* a surname, meaning elf or noble friend, used as a first name (*Old English*); a variant form is **Elwin**.

Elvina *fem* a variant form of **Elva**.

Elvira *fem* white (*Latin*).

Elvis *masc* wise one (*Norse*).

Elvy *masc* a variant form of **Elvey**.

Elwin *masc* a variant form of **Elvin**; white brow (*Welsh*); a variant form is **Elwyn**.

Emeline *fem* a variant form of **Amelia**; a diminutive form of **Emma**; a variant form is **Emmeline**.

Emerald *fem* the name of the green gemstone used as a first name.

Emery *masc* a variant form of **Amory**.

Emil *masc* of a noble Roman family the origin of whose name, *Aemilius*, is uncertain.

Émile *masc* the French form of **Emil**.

Emilia *fem* the Italian form of **Emily**.

Emilie *fem* the German form of **Emily**.

Émilie *fem* the French form of **Emily**.

Emilio *masc* the Italian, Spanish and Portuguese form of **Emil**.

Emily *fem* of a noble Roman family the origin of whose name, *Aemilius*, is uncertain.

Emlyn *masc* origin uncertain, possibly from **Emil** (*Welsh*).

Emma *fem* whole, universal (*Germanic*); diminutive forms are **Emm, Emmie**.

Emmanuel *masc* God with us (*Hebrew*); a variant form is **Immanuel**; a diminutive form is **Manny**.

Emmeline *fem* a variant form of **Emeline**.

Emmery *masc* a variant form of **Amory**.

Emmet, Emmett, Emmot, Emmott *masc* a surname, from a diminutive form of Emma, used as a first name.

Emory *masc* a variant form of **Amory**.

Emrys *masc* a Welsh form of **Ambrose**.

Emyr *masc* a Welsh form of **Honorius**.

Ena *fem* an anglicized form of **Eithne**.

Enda *fem* an anglicized form of **Éanna**.

Eneas *masc* a variant form of **Aeneas**.

Enée *masc* the French form of **Aeneas**.

Enfys *fem* rainbow (*Welsh*).

Engelbert *masc* bright angel (*Germanic*).

Engelberta, Engelbertha, Engelberthe *fem* forms of **Engelbert**.

Enid *fem* meaning uncertain, possibly woodlark (*Welsh*).

Ennis *masc* chief one (*Gaelic*).

Enoch *masc* consecrated; dedicated (*Hebrew*).

Enos *masc* man (*Hebrew*).

Enrica *fem* the Italian form of **Henrietta**.

Enrichetta *fem* the Italian form of **Henrietta**.

Enrico *masc* the Italian form of **Henry**.

Enrique *masc* the Spanish form of **Henry**.

Enriqueta *fem* the Spanish form of **Henrietta**.

Eoghan *masc* an Irish Gaelic form of **Eugene**.

Eoin *masc* an Irish form of **John**.

Ephraim *masc* very faithful (*Hebrew*); a diminutive form is **Eph**.

Eranthe *fem* Flower of spring (*Greek*).

Erasmus *masc* lovely; worthy of love (*Greek*); a diminutive form is **Ras, Rasmus**.

Erastus *masc* beloved; amiable (*Greek*); diminutive forms are **Ras, Rastus**.

Ercole *masc* the Italian form of **Hercules**.

Erda *fem* of the earth (*Germanic*).

Eric *masc* rich; brave; powerful (*Old English*); a variant form is **Erik**.

Erica *fem* form of **Eric**; a variant form is **Erika**.

Erich *masc* the German form of **Eric**.

Erik *masc* a variant form of **Eric**.

Erika *fem* a variant form of **Erica**.

Erin *fem* the poetic name for Ireland used as a first name.

Erland *masc* stranger (*Old Norse*).

Erle *masc* a variant form of **Earl**.

Erlene, Erline *fem* variant forms of **Earlene, Erline**; diminutive forms are **Erlie, Erley**.

Erma *fem* warrior maid (*Germanic*).

Ern *masc* a diminutive form of **Ernest**.

Erna *fem* a diminutive form of **Ernesta, Ernestine**.

Ernest *masc* earnest (*Germanic*); diminutive forms are **Ern, Ernie**.

Ernesta *fem* form of **Ernest**; a diminutive form is **Erna**.

Ernestine *fem* form of **Ernest**; diminutive forms are **Erna, Tina**.

Ernesto *masc* the Italian and Spanish forms of **Ernest**.

Ernst *masc* the German form of **Ernest**.

Erskine *masc* a placename and surname, meaning projecting height, used as a first name (*Scots Gaelic*).

Erwin *masc* friend of honour (*Germanic*); a surname, meaning wild-boar friend (*French*), used as a first name; a variant form is **Orwin**.

Eryl *masc* watcher (*Welsh*).

Esau *masc* hairy (*Hebrew*).

Esmé *masc, fem* beloved (*French*).

Esmeralda *fem* a Spanish form of **Emerald**.

Esmond *masc* divine protector (*Old English*).

Esta *fem* a variant form of **Esther**.

Este *masc* Man from the East (*Italian*).

Estéban *masc* the Spanish form of **Stephen**.

Estelle, Estella *fem* variant forms of **Stella**.

Ester *fem* the Italian and Spanish forms of **Esther**.

Esther *fem* star; good fortune; a secret (*Persian*); a variant form is **Esta**; diminutive forms are **Ess, Essie, Tess, Tessie**.

Estrella *fem* the Spanish form of **Estelle**.

Ethan *masc* firmness; strength (*Hebrew*).

Ethel *fem* noble; of noble birth (*Old English*).

Ethna *fem* an anglicized form of **Eithne**.

Etienne *masc* the French form of **Stephen**.

Etta, Ettie *fem* diminutive forms of **Henrietta**.

Ettore *masc* the Italian form of **Hector**.

Euan *masc* a variant form of **Ewan**.

Eudora *fem* good gift (*Greek*).

Eufemia *fem* the Italian and Spanish form of **Euphemia**.

Eugen *masc* the German form of **Eugene**.

Eugene *masc* well-born; noble (*Greek*); a diminutive form is **Gene**.

Eugène *masc* the French form of **Eugene**.

Eugenia *fem* form of **Eugene**; diminutive forms are **Ena, Gene**.

Eugénie *fem* the French form of **Eugenia**.

Eulalia *fem* fair speech (*Greek*).

Eunice *fem* happy victory (*Greek*).

Euphemia *fem* of good report (*Greek*); diminutive forms are **Fay, Effie, Phamie, Phemie**.

Eurig, Euros *masc* gold (*Welsh*).

Eusebio *masc* pious (*Greek*).

Eustace *masc* rich (*Greek*); diminutive forms are **Stacey, Stacy**.

Eustache *masc* the French form of **Eustace**.

Eustachio *masc* the Italian form of **Eustace**.

Eustacia *fem* form of **Eustace**; diminutive forms are
Stacey, Stacie, Stacy.

Eustaquio *masc* the Spanish form of **Eustace**.

Eva *fem* the German, Italian, and Spanish forms of **Eve**.

Evadne *fem* of uncertain meaning, possibly high-born
(*Greek*).

Evan *masc* young warrior (*Celtic*).

Evangeline *fem* bringer of good tidings (*Greek*).

Eve *fem* life (*Hebrew*); diminutive forms are **Evie, Eveli-
na, Eveline, Eveleen**.

Eveline *fem* a diminutive form of **Eva, Eve**.

Evelyn *masc fem* the English surname used as a first
name.

Everard *masc* strong as a wild boar (*Germanic*).

Everley *masc* Field of the wild boar (*Old English*).

Evita *fem* Spanish diminutive form of **Eva**.

Evodia *fem* good journey (*Greek*).

Ewan, Ewen *masc* Irish and Scots Gaelic forms of **Owen**;
a Scottish form of **Eugene**; a variant form is **Euan**.

Ewart *masc* an Old French variant of **Edward**; a surname, meaning herd of ewes used as a surname(*Old
English*).

Ezekiel *masc* strength of God (*Hebrew*); a diminutive
form is **Zeke**.

Ezra *masc* help (*Hebrew*).

F

Fabia *fem* form of **Fabio**; a variant form is **Fabiola**.

Fabian *masc* the anglicized form of the Roman family name *Fabianus*, derived from *Fabius*, from *faba*, bean (*Latin*).

Fabián *masc* the Spanish form of **Fabian**.

Fabiano *masc* the Italian form of **Fabian**.

Fabien *masc* the French form of **Fabian**.

Fabienne *fem* form of **Fabien**.

Fabio *masc* the Italian form of the Roman family name *Fabius*, from *faba*, bean.

Fabiola *fem* a variant form of **Fabia**.

Faber, Fabre *masc* a surname, meaning smith, used as a first name (*Latin*).

Fabrice *masc* the French form of the Roman family *Fabricius*, from *faber*, smith.

Fabrizio *masc* the Italian form of **Fabrice**.

Fairfax *masc* the surname, meaning lovely hair, used as a first name (*Old English*).

Fairley, Fairlie *masc* a surname, meaning clearing with ferns, used as a first name (*Old English*).

Faith *fem* the quality of belief or fidelity used as a first name.

Fanchon *fem* a diminutive form of **Françoise**.

Fane *masc* a surname, meaning glad or eager, used as a first name (*Old English*).

Fanny *fem* a diminutive form of **Frances**, also used independently.

Farnall, Farnell *masc* a surname, meaning fern hill, used as a first name(*Old English*); variant forms are **Fernald, Fernall**.

Farquhar *masc* dear man (*Scots Gaelic*).

Farr *masc* a surname, meaning bull, used as a first name (*Old English*).

Farrell *masc* warrior (*Irish Gaelic*).

Faustina, Faustine *fem* lucky (*Latin*).

Fatima *fem* the name of the daughter of Mohammed (*Semitic*); of Fatima in Portugal (*Portuguese*).

Favor, Favour *fem* an abstract noun, meaning good will or an act of good will, from *favere*, to protect, used as a first name (*Latin*).

Fawn *fem* the name for a young deer or a light greyish-brown colour used as a first name (*Old French*).

Fay, Faye *fem* faith or fairy (*Old French*); a diminutive form of **Euphemia**.

Federico *masc* an Italian and Spanish form of **Frederick**.

Felice *masc* the Italian form of **Felix**.

Felicia *fem* form of **Felix**.

Felicidad *fem* the Spanish form of **Felicia**.

Felicie *fem* the Italian form of **Felicia**.

Felicity *fem* happiness (*Latin*).

Felipe *masc* the Spanish form of **Philip**.

Felix *masc* happy (*Latin*).

Felton *masc* a placename and surname, meaning place in a field, used as a first name (*Old English*).

Fenella *fem* an anglicized form of **Fionnuala**.

Fenton *masc* a placename and surname, meaning a place in marshland or fens, used as a first name (*Old English*).

Ferdinand *masc* brave; valiant (*Germanic*); diminutive forms are **Ferd, Ferdy**.

Ferdinando *masc* an Italian form of **Ferdinand**.

Fergal *masc* man of strength (*Irish Gaelic*); diminutive forms are **Fergie, Fergy**.

Fergie *masc* a diminutive form of **Fergal, Fergus, Ferguson**; *fem* a diminutive form of **Ferguson** as a surname; a variant form is **Fergy**.

Fergus *masc* vigorous man (*Irish/Scots Gaelic*); diminutive forms are **Fergie, Fergy**.

Ferguson, Fergusson *masc* a surname, meaning son of Fergus, used as a first name; diminutive forms are **Fergie, Fergy**.

Fergy *masc*, *fem* a variant form of **Fergie**.

Fern *fem* the name of the plant used as a first name (*Old English*).

Fernald, Fernall *masc* variant forms of **Farnall, Farnell**.

Fernand *masc* a French form of **Ferdinand**.

Fernanda *fem* form of **Ferdnand**.

Fernando *masc* a Spanish form of **Ferdinand**.

Ffion *fem* foxglove (*Welsh*).

Fid *fem* a diminutive form of **Fidelia, Fidelis**.

Fidel *masc* a Spanish form of **Fidelis**.

Fidèle *masc* a French form of **Fidelis**.

Fidelia *fem* a variant form of **Fidelis**; a diminutive form is **Fid**.

Fidelio *masc* an Italian form of **Fidelis**.

Fidelis *masc, fem* faithful (*Latin*); a *fem* variant form is **Fidelia**; a diminutive form is **Fid**.

Fidelma *fem* faithful Mary (*Latin/Irish Gaelic*); a diminutive form is **Delma**.

Fielding *masc* a surname, meaning dweller in a field, used as a first name (*Old English*).

Fifi *fem* a French diminutive form of **Josephine**.

Filippo *masc* the Italian form of **Philip**.

Filippa *fem* the Italian form of **Philippa**.

Findlay *masc* a variant form of **Finlay**.

Fingal *masc* white stranger (*Scots Gaelic*).

Finlay, Finley *masc* fair warrior or calf (*Scots Gaelic*); a variant form is **Findlay**.

Finn *masc* fair, white (*Irish Gaelic*); a variant form is **Fionn**.

Finola *fem* a variant form of **Fionnuala**.

Fiona *fem* white, fair (*Scots Gaelic*).

Fionn *masc* a variant form of **Finn**.

Fionnuala *fem* white shoulder (*Irish Gaelic*); a diminutive form is **Nuala**, also used independently.

Fiske *masc* a surname, meaning fish, used as a first name (*Old English*).

Fitch *masc* a surname, meaning point, used as a first name (*Old English*).

Fitz *masc* son (*Old French*); a diminutive form of names beginning with Fitz-.

Fitzgerald *masc* a surname, meaning son of Gerald, used as a first name (*Old French*); a diminutive form is **Fitz**.

Fitzhugh *masc* a surname, meaning son of Hugh, used as a first name (*Old French*); a diminutive form is **Fitz**.

Fitzpatrick *masc* a surname, meaning son of Patrick, used as a first name (*Old French*); a diminutive form is **Fitz**.

Fitzroy *masc* a surname, meaning (illegitimate) son of the king, used as a first name (*Old French*); a diminutive form is **Fitz**.

Flann *masc* red-haired (*Irish Gaelic*).

Flanna *fem* form of **Flann**.

Flannan *masc* red-complexioned (*Irish Gaelic*).

Flavia *fem* yellow-haired, golden (*Latin*).

Flavian, Flavius *masc* forms of Flavia.

Fleming *masc* a surname, meaning man from Flanders, used as a first name (*Old French*).

Fletcher *masc* a surname meaning arrow-maker, used as a first name (*Old French*).

Fleur *fem* a flower (*French*).

Fleurette *fem* little flower (*French*).

Flinn *masc* a variant form of **Flynn**.

Flint *masc* stream, brook (*Old English*).

Flo *fem* a diminutive form of **Flora, Florence**.

Flora *fem* flowers; the Roman goddess of flowers (*Latin*); diminutive forms are **Flo, Florrie, Flossie**.

Florence *fem* blooming; flourishing (*Latin*); diminutive forms are **Flo, Florrie, Flossie, Floy**.

Florian *masc* flowering, blooming (*Latin*).

Florrie, Flossie *fem* diminutive forms of **Flora, Florence**.

Flower *fem* the English word for a bloom or blossom used as a first name.

Floy *fem* a diminutive form of **Flora, Florence**.

Floyd *masc* a variant form of the surname Lloyd used as a first name.

Flynn *masc* a surname, meaning son of the red-haired one, used as a first name (*Scots Gaelic*); a variant form is **Flinn**.

Forbes *masc* a placename and surname, meaning fields. or district, used as a first name (*Scots Gaelic*).

Ford *masc* the English word for a crossing place of a river used as a first name (*Old English*).

Forrest, Forrestt *masc* a surname, meaning forest, used as a first name (*Old French*).

Forrester, Forster *masc* a surname, meaning forester, used as a first name (*Old French*).

Fortune *fem* the word for wealth, fate or chance used as a first name (*Latin*); a variant form is **Fortuna**.

Foster *masc* a surname, meaning forester or cutler (*Old French*) or foster parent (*Old English*), used as a first name.

Fra *masc* a diminutive form of **Francis**.

Fraine *masc* a variant form of **Frayn**.

Fran *fem* a diminutive form of **Frances**.

Franca *fem* a diminutive form of **Francesca**.

Frances *fem* form of **Francis**; diminutive forms are **Fanny**, **Fran**, **Francie**.

Francesca *fem* the Italian form of **Frances**; a diminutive form is **Francheschina**.

Francesco *masc* the Italian form of **Francis**; a contracted form is **Franco**.

Francie *fem* a diminutive form of **Frances**.

Francine *fem* a diminutive form of **Frances, Françoise**.

Francis *masc* free (*Germanic*); diminutive forms are **Fra**, **Frank**, **Francie**.

Francisca *fem* the Spanish form of **Frances**.

Francisco *masc* the Spanish form of **Francis**.

Franco *masc* a contracted form of **Francesco**.

François *masc* the French form of **Francis**.

Françoise *fem* the French form of **Frances**.

Frank *masc* Frenchman (*Latin*); a diminutive form of **Francis**, **Franklin**; diminutive forms are **Frankie**, **Franky**.

Franklin, Franklen, Franklyn *masc* a surname, meaning free man, used as a first name (*Old French*); diminutive forms are **Frank, Frankie, Franky**.

Frans *masc* the Swedish form of **Francis**.

Franz, Franziskus *masc* German forms of **Francis**.

Franziska *masc* the German form of **Frances**.

Fraser, Frasier *masc* a Scottish surname, meaning from Frisselle or Fresel in France—possibly strawberry, used as a first name (*French*); variant forms are **Frazer, Frazier**.

Frayn, Frayne *masc* a surname, meaning ash tree, used as a surname (*Old French*); a variant form is **Fraine**.

Frazer, Frazier *masc* variant forms of **Fraser**.

Freda *fem* a diminutive form of **Winifred**; a variant form of **Frieda**.

Frédéric *masc* the French form of **Frederick**.

Frederica *fem* form of Frederick; diminutive forms are **Fred, Freddie, Freddy, Frieda**.

Frederick, Frederic *masc* abounding in peace; peaceful ruler (*Germanic*); diminutive forms are **Fred, Freddie, Freddy**.

Frédérique *fem* the French form of **Frederica**.

Fredrik *masc* the Swedish form of **Frederick**.

Freeman *masc* a surname, meaning free man, used as first name (*Old English*).

Frewin *masc* a surname, meaning generous friend, used as a first name (*Old English*).

Freya *fem* lady, the Norse goddess of love (*Norse*).

Frieda *fem* peace (*Germanic*); a diminutive form of **Frederica**.

Friede *fem* the German form of **Frieda**.

Friederike

Friederike *fem* the German form of **Frederica**; a diminutive form is **Fritzi**.

Friedrich *masc* German forms of **Frederick**; a diminutive form is **Fritz**.

Fritz *masc* a diminutive form of **Friedrich**, also used independently.

Fritzi *fem* a diminutive form of **Friederike**.

Fulton *masc* a surname, meaning muddy place, used as a first name (*Old English*).

Fulvia *fem* yellow-haired (*Latin*).

Fyfe, Fyffe *masc* a surname, meaning from Fife, used as a first name.

G

Gabe *masc* diminutive form of **Gabriel**.

Gabbie, Gabby *fem* diminutive forms of **Gabrielle**.

Gabriel *masc* strength of God; man of God; in the Bible one of the archangels (*Hebrew*); a diminutive form is **Gabe**.

Gabrielle *fem* form of **Gabriel**; diminutive forms are **Gabbie, Gabby**.

Gaea *fem* the Latin form of **Gaia**.

Gaia *fem* earth, in classical mythology the goddess of the earth (*Greek*); the Latin form is **Gaea**.

Gail *fem* a diminutive form of **Abigail**, now used independently; variant forms are **Gale, Gayle**.

Galatea *fem* white as milk, in Greek mythology a statue brought to life (*Greek*)

Gale *fem* a variant form of **Gail**; *masc* a surname, meaning jail, used as a first name (*Old French*).

Galen *masc* the anglicized form of the Roman family name *Galenus*, calmer (*Latin*).

Galia *fem* wave (*Hebrew*).

Gallagher *masc* a surname, meaning foreign helper, used as a first name (*Irish Gaelic*).

Galloway *masc* a placename and surname, meaning stranger Gaels, used as a first name (*Old Welsh*).

Galton *masc* a surname, meaning rented farm, used as a first name (*Old English*).

Galvin *masc* bright, white (*Irish Gaelic*).

Gamaliel *masc* recompense of God (*Hebrew*).

Gardenia *fem* the name of a flowering plant with fragrant flowers, called after Dr Alexander Garden, used as a first name (*New Latin*).

Gareth *masc* old man (*Welsh*); diminutive forms are **Gary, Garry**; a variant form is **Garth**.

Garfield *masc* a surname, meaning triangular piece of open land, used as a first name (*Old English*).

Garland *fem* the name for a wreath or crown of flowers used as a first name (*Old French*); *masc* a surname, meaning a maker of metal garlands, used as a first name (*Old English*).

Garnet *fem* the name of a deep-red gemstone used as a first name (*Old French*).

Garnet, Garnett *masc* a surname, meaning pomegranate, used as a first name (*Old French*).

Garret, Garrett *masc* the Irish Gaelic form of **Gerard**; a variant form of **Garrard**.

Garrard *masc* a variant form of **Gerard**.

Garrison *masc* a surname, meaning son of Garret, used as a first name (*Old English*).

Garry *masc* a variant form of **Gary**; a placename, meaning rough water, used as a first name (*Scots Gaelic*).

Garth *masc* a surname, meaning garden or paddock, used as a first name (*Old Norse*); a variant form of **Gareth**.

Garton *masc* a surname, meaning fenced farm, used as a first name (*Old Norse*).

Garve *masc* a placename, meaning rough place, used as a first name (*Scots Gaelic*).

Gary *masc* spear carrier (*Germanic*); a diminutive form of **Gareth**; a variant form is **Garry**.

Gaspard *masc* the French form of **Jasper**.

Gaston *masc* stranger, guest (*Germanic*); from Gascony (*Old French*).

Gautier, Gauthier *masc* French forms of **Walter**.

Gavin *masc* an anglicized form of **Gawain**.

Gawain *masc* white hawk (*Welsh*).

Gay *fem* an English adjective, meaning being joyous used as a first name (*Old French*); *masc* an Irish diminutive form of **Gabriel**.

Gayle *fem* a variant form of **Gail**.

Gaylord *masc* a surname, meaning brisk noble man, used as a first name (*Old French*).

Gaynor *fem* a medieval English form of **Guinevere**.

Gazella *fem* like a gazelle or antelope (*Latin*).

Gemma *fem* the Italian word for a gem used as a first name; a variant form is **Jemma**.

Gene *masc* a diminutive form of **Eugene**, now used independently.

Geneva *fem* a variant form of **Genevieve**; the name of a Swiss city used as a first name.

Genevieve *fem* meaning uncertain, possibly tribe woman (*Celtic*).

Geneviève *fem* the French form of **Genevieve**.

Geoffrey *masc* a variant form of **Jeffrey**; a diminutive form is **Geoff**.

Georg *masc* the German form of **George**.

George *masc* a landholder; husbandman (*Germanic*); diminutive forms are **Geordie, Georgie, Georgy**.

Georges *masc* the French form of **George**.

Georgia, Georgiana, Georgina *fem* forms of **George**; a diminutive form is **Georgie**.

Geraint *masc* old man (*Welsh*).

Gerald *masc* strong with the spear (*Germanic*); diminutive forms are **Gerrie, Gerry, Jerry**.

Geraldine *fem* form of **Gerald**.

Gerard *masc* firm spear (*Old German*); variant forms are **Garrard, Garratt, Gerrard**; diminutive forms are **Gerrie, Gerry, Jerry**.

Gérard *masc* the French form of **Gerard**.

Gerardo *masc* the Italian form of **Gerard**.

Géraud *masc* a French form of **Gerald**.

Gerhard *masc* the German form of **Gerard**.

Gerhold *masc* a German form of **Gerald**.

Germain *masc* brother (*Latin*); diminutive forms are **Gerrie, Gerry**.

Germaine *fem* form of **Germain**; a variant form is **Jermaine**.

Geronimo, Gerolamo *masc* Italian forms of **Jerome**.

Gerrie, Gerry *masc* diminutive forms of **Gerald, Gerard**; *fem* a diminutive form of **Geraldine**.

Gershom *masc* an exile (*Hebrew*).

Gertrude *fem* spear maiden (*Germanic*); diminutive forms are **Gert, Gertie, Trudi, Trudy**.

Gervas *masc* the German form of **Gervase**.

Gervase, Gervaise *masc* spearman (*Germanic*); variant forms are **Gervaise, Jarvis, Jervis**.

Gervais *masc* the French form of **Gervase**.

Gervaise *masc* a variant form of **Gervase**.

Gervasio *masc* the Italian, Portuguese and Spanish form of **Gervase**.

Gethin *masc* dusky (*Welsh*).

Giacomo *masc* an Italian form of **James**.

Gian, Gianni *masc* diminutive forms of **Giovanni**.

Gibson *masc* a surname, meaning son of Gilbert, used as a first name (*Old English*).

Gideon *masc* a destroyer (*Hebrew*).

Giffard, Gifford *masc* a surname, meaning bloated (*Old French*) or gift (*Germanic*).

Gigi *fem* a French diminutive form of **Georgine, Virginie**.

Gil *masc* a diminutive form of **Gilbert, Gilchrist, Giles**; a Spanish form of **Giles**.

Gilbert *masc* yellow-bright; famous (*Germanic*); diminutive form is **Gil**.

Gilberta, Gilberte *fem* forms of **Gilbert**; diminutive forms are **Gill, Gillie, Gilly**.

Gilchrist *masc* servant of Christ (*Scots Gaelic*); a diminutive form is **Gil**.

Gilda *fem* sacrifice (*Germanic*).

Giles *masc* a kid (*Greek*); a diminutive form is **Gil**.

Gill *fem* a diminutive form of **Gilberta, Gilberte, Gillian**.

Gilles *masc* the French form of **Giles**.

Gillespie *masc* a surname, meaning servant of a bishop, used as a first name (*Scots Gaelic*).

Gillie *fem* a diminutive form of **Gilberta, Gilberte, Gillian**.

Gillian *fem* form of **Julian**; diminutive forms are **Gill, Gillie, Gilly**.

Gillmore *masc* a variant form of **Gilmore**.

Gilly *fem* a diminutive form of **Gilberta, Gilberte, Gillian**.

Gilmore, Gilmour *masc* a surname, meaning servant of St Mary, used as a first name (*Scots Gaelic*); a variant form is **Gillmore**.

Gilroy *masc* a surname, meaning servant of the red haired one, used as a first name (*Gaelic*).

Gina *fem* a diminutive form of **Georgina**, also used independently.

Ginnie, Ginny *fem* a diminutive form of **Virginia**.

Gioacchino *masc* the Italian form of **Joachim**.

Giorgio *masc* the Italian form of **George**.

Giovanna *fem* the Italian form of **Jane**.

Giovanni *masc* the Italian form of **John**; diminutive forms are **Gian, Gianni**.

Gipsy *fem* a variant form of **Gypsy**.

Giraldo *masc* the Italian form of **Gerald**.

Giraud, Girauld *masc* French forms of **Gerald**.

Girolamo *masc* an Italian form of **Jerome**.

Girvan *masc* a placename, meaning short river, used as a first name (*Scots Gaelic*).

Giselle *fem* promise, pledge (*Germanic*)

Gisela *fem* the Dutch and German form of **Giselle**.

Gisèle *fem* the French form of **Giselle**.

Gitana *fem* gipsy (*Spanish*).

Giulio *masc* the Italian form of **Julius**.

Giuseppe *masc* the Italian form of **Joseph**; a diminutive form is **Beppe, Beppo**.

Gladwin *masc* a surname, meaning glad friend, used as a first name (*Old English*).

Gladys *fem* the anglicized Welsh form of **Claudia**.

Glanville *masc* Dweller on the oak tree estate (*French*); a diminutive form is **Glanvil**.

Gleda *fem* Old English version of Gladys (*Old English*).

Glen *masc* the surname, meaning a valley, used as a first name (*Scots Gaelic*); a variant form is **Glenn**.

Glenda *fem* clean and good (*Welsh*); a variant form is **Glenys**.

Glendon *masc* From the fortress in the Glen (*Celtic*).

Glenn *masc* a variant form of **Glen**, now also used as a feminine name.

Glenna *fem* form of **Glen**.

Glenys *fem* a variant form of **Glenda**; a variant form is **Glynis**.

Gloria *fem* glory (*Latin*).

Glyn *masc* valley (*Welsh*); a variant form is **Glynn**.

Glynis *fem* form of **Glyn**; a variant form of **Glenys**.

Glynn *masc* a variant form of **Glyn**.

Goddard *masc* pious; virtuous (*Old German*).

Godfrey *masc* at peace with God (*Germanic*).

Godiva *fem* gift of God (*Old English*)**u**.

Godwin *masc* God's friend (*Old English*).

Golda, Golde *fem* gold (*Yiddish*).

Goldie *fem* an anglized form of **Golda**; fair-haired (*English*).

Golding *masc* a surname, meaning son of gold, used as a first name (*Old English*).

Goldwin *masc* Golden friend (*Old English*).

Goodwin *masc* a surname, meaning good friend, used as a first name; (*Old English*).

Gordon *masc* a surname, meaning great hill, used as a first name (*Scots Gaelic*).

Gottfried *masc* the German form of **Godfrey**; a diminutive form is **Götz**.

Grace *fem* grace (*Latin*); a diminutive form is **Gracie**.

Grady *masc* a surname, meaning noble, used as a first name (*Irish Gaelic*).

Graham, Grahame, Graeme *masc* a Scottish surname, meaning gravelly homestead, used as a first name (*Old English*).

Gráinne *fem* love (*Irish Gaelic*).

Granger *masc* a surname, meaning farmer or bailiff, used as a first name (*Old English*).

Grant *masc* a surname, meaning large, used as a first name (*Norman French*).

Granville *masc* large town (*Old French*).

Gray *masc* a surname, meaning grey-haired, used as a first name (*Old English*); a variant form is **Grey**.

Greeley *masc* a surname, meaning pitted, used as a first name (*Old English*).

Greer *fem* form of the surname **Grier**.

Grégoire *masc* the French form of **Gregory**.

Gregor *masc* a Scots form of **Gregory**.

Gregorio *masc* the Italian and Spanish form of **Gregory**.

Gregory *masc* watchful; vigilant (*Greek*); a diminutive form is **Greg**.

Gresham *masc* a surname, meaning grazing meadow, used as a first name (*Old English*).

Greta *fem* a diminutive form of **Margaret**.

Gretchen *fem* a diminutive form of **Margaret, Margarete**.

Grete *fem* a diminutive form of **Margarete**.

Greville *masc* a surname, meaning from Gréville in France, used as a first name.

Grier *masc*, *fem* a surname, a contracted form of **Gregor**, used as a first name; a variant *fem* form is **Greer**.

Griff *masc* a diminutive form of **Griffin, Griffith**.

Griffin *masc* a Latinized form of **Griffith**; a diminutive form is **Griff**.

Griffith *masc* an anglicized form of **Gruffydd**; a diminutive form is **Griff**.

Griselda, Grizelda *fem* stone heroine (*Germanic*); diminutive forms are **Grissel, Grizel, Grizzel**.

Grover *masc* a surname, meaning from a grove of trees, used as a first name (*Old English*).

Gruffydd *masc* powerful chief (*Welsh*).

Gualterio *masc* the Spanish form of **Walter**.

Gualtieri *masc* the Italian form of **Walter**.

Gudrun *fem* God's secret (*Old Norse*)a.

Guglielmo *masc* the Italian form of **William**.

Guido *masc* the German, Italian, and Spanish forms of **Guy**.

Guilbert *masc* a French form of **Gilbert**.

Guillaume *masc* the French form of **William**.

Guillermo, Guillelmo *masc* Spanish forms of **William**.

Guinevere *fem* white and soft, the name of the wife of King Arthur (*Welsh*).

Gunhilda, Gunhilde *fem* warrior maid (*Old Norse*).

Gunnar *masc* the Scandinavian form of **Gunter**.

Gunter *masc* battle warrior (*Germanic*).

Günther *masc* the German form of **Gunter**.

Gus *masc* a diminutive form of **Angus, Augustus, Gustave**.

Gussie, Gusta *fem* diminutive forms of **Augusta**.

Gustaf *masc* the Swedish form of **Gustave**.

Gustave *masc* staff of the Goths (*Swedish*); a diminutive form is **Gus**.

Guthrie *masc* a surname, meaning windy, used as a first name (*Scots Gaelic*).

Guy *masc* a leader (*German-French*).

Guyon *masc* a French form of **Guy**.

Gwenda *fem* a diminutive form of **Gwendolen**, also used independently.

Gwendolen, Gwendolin, Gwendolyn *fem* white ring or bow (*Welsh*); diminutive forms are **Gwen, Gwenda, Gwennie**.

Gwillym, Gwilym *masc* Welsh forms of **William**.

Gwyneth *fem* blessed (*Welsh*).

Gwyn, Gwynn *masc* fair, blessed (*Welsh*); diminutive forms are **Gwyn, Guin**.

Gwynfor *masc* fair lord (*Welsh*).

Gypsy *fem* the name for a member of a people who live a nomadic life used as a first name; a variant form is **Gipsy**.

H

Haakon *masc* a variant form of **Hakon**.

Hackett *masc* a surname, meaning little woodcutter, used as a first name (*Old Norse*).

Haddan, Hadden, Haddon *masc* a surname, meaning heathery hill, used as a first name (*Old English*).

Hadley *masc* a surname, meaning heathery hill or heathery meadow, used as a first name (*Old English*).

Hadrian *masc* a variant form of **Adrian**.

Hagar *fem* flight (*Hebrew*).

Hagan, Hagan *masc* young Hugh (*Irish Gaelic*); thorn bush or thorn fence (*Germanic*).

Hagley *masc* a surname, meaning haw wood or clearing, used as a first name (*Old English*).

Haidee *fem* modest, honoured (*Greek*); a variant form of **Heidi**.

Haig *masc* a first name, meaning one who lives in an enclosure, used as a first name (*Old English*).

Hakon *masc* from the exalted race (*Old Norse*); a variant form is **Haakon**; a diminutive form is **Hako**.

Hal *masc* a diminutive form of **Halbert, Henry**.

Halbert *masc* brilliant hero (*Old English*); a diminutive form is **Hal**.

Halcyon, Halcyone *fem* variant forms of **Alcyone**.

Haldan, Haldane, Halden, Haldin *fem* a surname, meaning half Dane, used as a surname (*Old English*).

Hale *masc* a surname, meaning from the hall, used as a surname (*Old English*).

Haley *masc, fem* a variant form of **Hayley**.

Halford *masc* a surname, meaning from a ford in a hollow, used as a first name (*Old English*).

Haliwell *masc* a variant form of **Halliwell**.

Hall *masc* a surname, meaning one who lives at a manor house, used as a first name (*Old English*).

Hallam *masc* a surname, meaning at the hollow (*Old English*), or a placename, meaning at the rocky place (*Old Norse*), used as a first name.

Halliwell *masc* a surname, meaning one who lives by the holy well, used as a first name (*Old English*); a variant form is **Haliwell**.

Halstead, Halsted *masc* a surname, meaning from the stronghold, used as a first name (*Old English*).

Halton *masc* a surname, meaning from the lookout hill, used as a first name (*Old English*).

Hamar *masc* strong man (*Old Norse*).

Hamilton *masc* a surname, meaning farm in broken country, used as a first name. (*Old English*).

Hamish *masc* a Scots Gaelic form of **James**.

Hamlet, Hamlett *masc* a surname, meaning little home, used as a first name (*Germanic*).

Hammond *masc* a surname, meaning belonging to Hamon, used as a first name (*Old English*).

Hamon *masc* great protection (*Old English*).

Hanford *masc* a surname, meaning rocky ford or ford with cocks, used as a first name (*Old English*).

Hank *masc* a diminutive form of **Henry**.

Hanley *masc* a surname, meaning from the high meadow or hill, used as a first name (*Old English*).

Hannah *fem* grace (*Hebrew*); a variant form is **Ann**; a diminutive form is **Nana**.

Hannibal *masc* grace of Baal (*Punic*).

Hans *masc* a diminutive form of **Johann**.

Hansel *masc* gift from God (*Scandinavian*).

Happy *fem* an English adjective, meaning feeling, showing or expressing joy, now used as a first name (*Old English*).

Haralda *fem* form of **Harold**.

Harbert *masc* a variant form of **Herbert**.

Harcourt *masc* a surname, meaning from a fortified court (*Old French*), or falconer's cottage (*Old English*), used as a first name.

Harden *masc* a surname, meaning the valley of the hare, used as a first name (*Old English*).

Hardie, Hardey *masc* variant forms of **Hardy**.

Harding *masc* a surname, meaning brave warrior, used as a first name (*Old English*).

Hardy *masc* a surname, meaning bold and daring, used as a first name (*Germanic*); variant forms are **Hardey, Hardie**.

Harford *masc* a surname, meaning stags' ford, used as a first name (*Old English*).

Hargrave, Hargreave, Hargreaves *masc* a surname, meaning from the hare grove, used as a first name (*Old English*).

Harlan, Harland *masc* a surname, meaning rocky land, used as a first name (*Old English*).

Harley *masc* a surname, meaning from the hare meadow or hill, used as a first name (*Old English*).

Harlow *masc* a placename and surname, meaning fortified hill, used as a first name (*Old English*).

Harmony *fem* the word for the quality of concord used as a first name (*Greek*).

Harold *masc* a champion; general of an army (*Old English*).

Harper *masc* a surname, meaning harp player or maker, used as a first name (*Old English*).

Harriet, Harriot *fem* forms of **Harry**; diminutive forms are **Hattie, Hatty**.

Harris, Harrison *masc* surnames, meaning son of Harold or Harry, used as a first name (*Old English*)

Harry *masc* a diminutive form of **Henry**, also used independently.

Hart *masc* a surname, meaning hart deer, used as a first name (*Old English*).

Hartford *masc* a placename and surname, meaning ford of the deer, or army ford, used as a first name (*Old English*); a variant form is **Hertford**.

Hartley *masc* a surname, meaning clearing with stags, used as a first name (*Old English*).

Hartmann, Hartman *masc* strong and brave (*Germanic*).

Hartwell *masc* a surname, meaning stags' stream, used as a first name (*Old English*).

Harvey, Harvie *masc* a surname, meaning battle worthy, used as a first name (*Breton Gaelic*); a variant form is **Hervey**.

Haslett, Hazlitt *masc* variant forms of **Hazlett**.

Hastings *masc* a placename and surname, meaning territory of the violent ones, used as a first name (*Old English*).

Hattie *fem* a diminutive form of **Harriet**.

Havelock *masc* a surname, meaning sea battle, used as a first name (*Old Norse*).

Hawley *masc* a surname, meaning from a hedged meadow, used as a first name (*Old English*).

Hayden, Haydon *masc* a surname, meaning heather hill or hay hill, used as a first name (*Old English*).

Hayley *masc, fem* a surname, meaning hay clearing, used as a first name (*Old English*); a variant form is **Haley**.

Hayward *masc* a surname, meaning supervisor of enclosures, used as a first name (*Old English*); a variant form is **Heyward**.

Haywood *masc* a surname, meaning fenced forest, used as a first name (*Old English*); a variant form is **Heywood**.

Hazel *fem* the name of a tree used as a first name (*Old English*).

Hazlett, Hazlitt *masc* a surname, meaning hazel tree, used as a first name (*Old English*); variant forms are **Haslett, Hazlitt**.

Heath *masc* a surname, meaning heathland, used as a first name (*Old English*).

Heathcliff, Heathcliffe *masc* dweller by the heather cliff (*Old English*).

Heather *fem* the name of a purple or white-flowered plant of the heath family used as a first name.

Hebe *fem* young (*Greek*). In Greek mythology, the daughter of Zeus and goddess of youth and spring.

Hector *masc* holding fast (*Greek*).

Hedda *fem* war, strife (*Germanic*).

Hedwig, Hedvig *fem* strife (*Germanic*).

Hefin *masc* summery (*Welsh*).

Heidi *fem* diminutive of **Adelheid**; a variant form is **Haidee**.

Heinrich *masc* the German form of **Henry**; diminutive forms are **Heinz, Heinze**.

Helen, Helena *fem* light (*Greek*); diminutive forms are **Nell, Lena**.

Helene *fem* the German form of **Helen**.

Hélène *fem* the French form of **Helen**.

Helga *fem* healthy, happy, holy (*Old Norse*).

Helge *masc* form of **Helga**.

Helma *fem* protection (*Germanic*).

Héloïse *fem* a French variant form of **Éloise**.

Hendrik *masc* the Dutch form of **Henry**.

Henri *masc* the French form of **Henry**.

Henrietta *fem* form of **Henry**; diminutive forms are **Hettie, Hetty, Netta, Nettie**.

Henriette *fem* the French form of **Henrietta**.

Henry *masc* the head or chief of a house (*Germanic*); diminutive forms are **Harry, Hal, Hank**.

Hephzibah *fem* my delight is in her (*Hebrew*); a diminutive form is **Hepsy**.

Hera *fem* queen of heaven; in Greek mythology, the sister and wife of Zeus (*Greek*). Her counterpart in Roman mythology is Juno.

Herakles *masc* the Greek counterpart of **Hercules**.

Herbert *masc* glory of the army (*Old English*); a variant form is **Harbert**; diminutive forms are **Herb, Herbie**.

Hercule *masc* the French form of **Hercules**.

Hercules *masc* glory of Hera (the Latin form of the name of Herakles, the Greek hero, son of Zeus and stepson of Hera).

Heribert *masc* the German form of **Herbert**.

Herman *masc* warrior (*Germanic*).

Hermann *masc* the German form of **Herman**.

Hermes *masc* in Greek mythology, the messenger of the gods, with winged feet. His counterpart in Roman mythology is Mercury.

Hermione *fem* a name derived from that of **Hermes**.

Hermosa *fem* beautiful (*Spanish*).

Hernando *masc* a Spanish form of **Ferdinand**.

Herrick *masc* a surname, meaning powerful ruler, used as a first name (*Old Norse*).

Herta *fem* of the earth (*Old English*); a variant form is **Hertha**.

Hertford *masc* a variant form of **Hartford**.

Hertha *fem* a variant form of **Herta**.

Hervé *masc* a French form of **Harvey**.

Hervey *masc* a variant form of **Harvey**.

Hesketh *masc* a surname, meaning horse track, used as a first name (*Old Norse*).

Hester, Hesther *fem* variant forms of **Esther**.

Hettie, Hetty *fem* diminutive forms of **Henrietta**.

Heulwen *fem* sunshine (*Welsh*).

Hew *masc* a Welsh form of **Hugh**.

Hewett, Hewit *masc* a surname, meaning little Hugh or cleared place, used as a first name (*Old English*).

Heyward *masc* a variant form of **Hayward**.

Heywood *masc* a variant form of **Haywood**.

Hezekiah *masc* strength of the Lord (*Hebrew*).

Hi *masc* a diminutive form of **Hiram, Hyram**.

Hibernia *fem* the Latin name for Ireland used as a first name.

Hibiscus *fem* marsh mallow, the name of a brightly flowering plant used as a first name (*Greek/Latin*).

Hieronymus *masc* the Latin and German forms of **Jerome**.

Hilaire *masc* the French form of **Hilary**.

Hilario *masc* the Spanish form of **Hilary**.

Hilary, Hillary *masc fem* cheerful; merry (*Latin*).

Hilda *fem* battle maid (*Germanic*); a variant form is **Hylda**.

Hildebrand *masc* battle sword (*Germanic*).

Hildegarde *fem* strong in battle (*Germanic*).

Hilton *masc* a surname, meaning from the hill farm, used as a first name (*Old English*); a variant form is **Hylton**.

Hiram *masc* most noble (*Hebrew*); a variant form is **Hyram**; a diminutive form is **Hi**.

Hobart *masc* a variant form of **Hubert**.

Hogan *masc* youthful (*Irish Gaelic*).

Holbert, Holbird *masc* variant forms of **Hulbert**.

Holbrook *masc* a surname, meaning brook in the valley, used as a first name (*Old English*).

Holcomb, Holcombe *masc* a surname, meaning deep valley, used as a first name (*Old English*).

Holden *masc* a surname, meaning from the deep valley, used as a first name (*Old English*).

Holgate *masc* a surname, meaning road in a hollow, used as a first name (*Old English*).

Hollis *masc* a surname, meaning dweller near holly trees, used as a first name (*Old English*).

Holly, Hollie *fem* the name of the red-berried tree used as a first name (*English*).

Holmes *masc* a surname, meaning an island in a river, used as a first name (*Old English*).

Holt *masc* a surname, meaning a wood or forest, used as a first name (*Old English*).

Homer *masc* uncertain, possibly hostage (*Greek*); the name of the Greek epic poet of the first milennium BC.

Honey *fem* the word for a sweet substance used as a term of endearment and as a first name.

Honor, Honora *fem* variant forms of **Honour**.

Honoria *fem* honourable (*Latin*); diminutive forms are **Nora, Norah, Noreen**.

Honorius *masc* form of **Honoria**.

Honour *fem* the word for personal intregity used as a first name; variant forms are **Honor, Honora**.

Hope *fem* the word for the feeling of expectation used as a first name (*English*).

Horace, Horatio *masc* origin uncertain, possibly a family name *Horatius* (*Latin*).

Horatia *fem* form of **Horace**.

Hortensia, Hortense *fem* a lady in the garden (*Latin*).

Horton *masc* a surname, meaning muddy place, used as a first name (*Old English*).

Hosea *masc* salvation (*Hebrew*).

Houghton *masc* a surname, meaning place in an enclosure, used as a first name (*Old English*); a variant form is **Hutton**.

Houston, Houstun *masc* a surname, meaning Hugh's place, used as a first name (*Old English*).

Howard *masc* a surname, meaning high warden, used as a first name (*Germanic*).

Howe *masc* a surname, meaning high one (*Germanic*) or hill (*Old English*) used as a first name.

Howel, Howell *masc* anglicized forms of **Hywel**.

Hubert *masc* bright in spirit; soul-bright (*Germanic*); a variant surname form is **Hobart**.

Huberta *fem* form of **Hubert**.

Hudson *masc* a surname, meaning son of little Hugh, used as a first name (*Old English*).

Hugh *masc* mind; spirit; soul (*Danish*).

Hugo *masc* the Latin, German, and Spanish form of **Hugh**.

Hugues *masc* the French form of **Hugh**.

Hulbert, Hulburd, Hulburt *masc* a surname, meaning brilliant, gracious, used as a first name (*Germanic*); variant forms are **Holbert, Holbird**.

Hulda, Huldah *fem* weasel (*Hebrew*).

Humbert *masc* bright warrior (*Germanic*).

Humphrey, Humphry *masc* protector of the home (*Old English*); diminutive forms are **Hump, Humph**.

Hunt, Hunter *masc* surnames, meaning hunter, used as first names (*Old English*).

Huntingdon *masc* a placename and surname, meaning hunter's hill, used as a first name (*Old English*).

Huntington *masc* a surname, meaning hunter's farm, used as a first name (*Old English*).

Huntley, Huntly *masc* a surname, meaning hunter's meadow, used as a first name (*Old English*).

Hurley *masc* Sea tide (*Gaelic*).

Hurst *masc* a surname, meaning wooded hill, used as a first name (*Old English*).

Hutton *masc* a variant form of **Houghton**.

Huw *masc* a Welsh variant form of **Hugh**.

Huxley *masc* a surname, meaning Hugh's meadow, used as a first name (*Old English*).

Hyacinth *fem* the name of the flower adapted from the name of the hero of Greek mythology whose blood after his killing by Apollo caused a flower to spring up.

Hyam *masc* man of life (*Hebrew*); a variant form is **Hyman**; diminutive forms are **Hi, Hy**.

Hyde *masc* a surname, meaning a hide (a measurement unit) of land, used as a first name (*Old English*).

Hylda *fem* a variant form of **Hilda**.

Hylton *masc* a variant form of **Hilton**.

Hyman *masc* a variant form of **Hyam**.

Hypatia *fem* highest (*Greek*).

Hyram *masc* a variant form of **Hiram**; diminutive forms are **Hi, Hy**.

Hywel, Hywell *masc* sound; whole (*Welsh*); anglicized forms are **Howel, Howell**.

I

Iachimo *masc* an Italian form of **James**.

Iacovo *masc* an Italian form of **Jacob**.

Ian *masc* an anglicized form of **Iain**.

Iain *masc* the Scots Gaelic form of **John**.

Ianthe *fem* violet flower (*Greek*).

Ibby *fem* a diminutive form of **Isabel**.

Ichabod *masc* the glory has departed (*Hebrew*).

Ida *fem* god-like (*Germanic*).

Idabell *fem* god-like and fair.

Idris *masc* fiery lord (*Welsh*).

Idony, Idonie *fem* in Norse mythology, the keeper of the golden apples of youth (*Norse*).

Iestyn *masc* the Welsh form of **Justin**.

Ieuan, Ifan *masc* Welsh forms of **John**; a variant form is **Iwan**.

Ifor *masc* a Welsh form of **Ivor**.

Ignace *masc* the French form of **Ignatius**.

Ignacio *masc* a Spanish form of **Ignatius**.

Ignatia *fem* form of **Ignatius**.

Ignatius *masc* ardent; fiery (*Greek*).

Ignatz, Ignaz *masc* German forms of **Ignatius**.

Ignazio *masc* the Italian form of **Ignatius**.

Igor *masc* the Russian form of **Ivor**.

Ike *masc* a diminutive form of **Isaac**.

Ilario *masc* the Italian form of **Hilary**.

Ilona *fem* a Hungarian form of **Helen**; a diminutive form is **Ilka**.

Ilse *fem* a diminutive form of **Elisabeth**.

Immanuel *masc* a variant form of Emmanuel; a diminutive form is **Manny**.

Imogen *fem* from *Innogen*, "girl, maiden" (*Celtic*), used by Shakespeare for one of his characters in *Cymbeline* and misspelled by him or his printer.

Imperial *fem* relating to an emperor (*Latin*).

Imre *masc* a Hungarian form of **Emeric**.

Ina *fem* a diminutive form of names ending in *-ina*, e.g. Georgina, Wilhelmina.

Inés, Inez *fem* Spanish forms of **Agnes**.

Inga *fem* a diminutive form of **Ingeborg, Ingrid**.

Inge *masc* a diminutive form of **Ingemar**; *fem* a diminutive form of **Ingeborg, Ingrid**.

Ingeborg *fem* fortification of Ing, the god of fertility (Frey) (*Old Norse*); diminutive forms are **Inga, Inge**.

Ingemar *masc* famous son of Ing (*Old Norse*); a variant form is **Ingmar**; a diminutive form is **Inge**.

Inger *fem* a variant form of **Ingrid**.

Ingmar *masc* a variant form of **Ingemar**.

Ingram *masc* a surname, meaning raven angel (*Germanic*) or river meadow (*Old English*), used as a first name.

Ingrid *fem* maiden of Ing, the god of fertility (Frey) (*Old Norse*); a variant form is **Inger**; diminutive forms are **Inga, Inge**.

Inigo *masc* a Spanish form of **Ignatius**, now used as an English-language form.

Innes, Inness *masc, fem* a surname, meaning island, used as a first name (*Scots Gaelic*).

Iola *fem* a variant form of **Iole**.

Iolanthe *fem* violet flower (*Greek*).

Iole *fem* violet (*Greek*); a variant form is **Iola**.

Iolo, Iolyn *masc* diminutive forms of **Iorwerth**.

Iona *fem* yew tree (*Celtic*), the name of the Scottish Hebridean island used as a first name.

Iorwerth *masc* handsome nobleman (*Welsh*); diminutive forms are **Iolo, Iolyn**.

Iphigenia *fem* strong (*Greek*).

Ira *masc* watchful (*Hebrew*).

Irene *fem* peace (*Greek*); a diminutive form is **Renie**.

Iris *fem* rainbow (*Greek*).

Irma *fem* noble one (Germanic).

Irvine, Irving *masc* a surname, meaning fresh or green river, used as a first name (*Celtic*).

Irwin *masc* a surname, meaning friend of boars, used as a first name (*Old English*).

Isa *fem* a diminutive form of **Isabel**.

Isaac *masc* laughter (*Hebrew*); a variant form is **Izaak**; a diminutive form is **Ike**.

Isabel, Isabella *fem* Spanish forms of **Elizabeth**, now

used as separate English-language names; a variant
form is **Isobel**; diminutive forms are **Ibby, Isa, Izzie,
Izzy, Tib, Tibbie**.

Isabelle *fem* the French form of **Isabel**.

Isadora *fem* a variant form of **Isidora**.

Isaiah *masc* salvation of the Lord (*Hebrew*).

Iseabail, Ishbel *fem* Scots forms of **Isabel**.

Iseult *fem* a French and Welsh form of **Isolde**.

Isham *masc* a surname, meaning home on the water, used
as a first name (*Old English*).

Isidor *masc* the German form of **Isidore**.

Isidora *fem* form of **Isidore**; a variant form is **Isadora** .

Isidore *masc* gift of Isis (*Greek*).

Isidoro *masc* an Italian form of **Isidore**.

Isidro *masc* Spanish forms of **Isidore**.

Isla *fem* a Scottish river name used as a first name.

Isobel *fem* a variant form of **Isabel**.

Isola *fem* isolated, alone (*Latin*).

Isolde, Isolda *fem* beautiful aspect (*Welsh*).

Israel *masc* a soldier of God ruling with the Lord (*Hebrew*); a diminutive form is **Izzy**.

Istvan *masc* the Hungarian form of Stephen.

Ita, Ite *fem* thirst (for truth) (*Irish Gaelic*).

Ivan *masc* the Russian form of **John**.

Ivana *fem* form of **Ivan**.

Ives *masc* a surname, meaning son of Ive (yew), used as
a first name (*Germanic*).

Ivo *masc* the Welsh form of **Yves**.

Ivor

Ivor *masc* yew army (*Old Norse*).
Ivy *masc fem* the name of the plant used as a first name
    (*English*).
Iwan *masc* a variant form of **Ieuan**.
Izaak *masc* a variant form of **Isaac**.
Izzie, Izzy *masc fem* diminutive forms of **Isabel, Israel**.

J

Jabal *masc* guide (*Hebrew*).

Jabez *masc* he will cause pain (*Hebrew*).

Jacinta *fem* the Spanish form of **Hyacinth**.

Jacinth *fem* a variant form of **Hyacinth**.

Jack *masc* a diminutive form of **John**, now used independently; diminutive forms are **Jackie, Jacky**.

Jackie, Jacky *masc* a diminutive form of **Jack, John**; *fem* a diminutive form of **Jacqueline**.

Jackson *masc* a surname, meaning son of Jack, used as a first name.

Jacob *masc* a supplanter (*Hebrew*); a diminutive form is **Jake**.

Jacoba *fem* fem form of **Jacob**.

Jacobo *masc* the Spanish form of **Jacob**.

Jacqueline *fem* a diminutive form of **Jacques**; a variant form is **Jaqueline**; a diminutive form is **Jackie**.

Jacques *masc* the French form of **Jacob, James**.

Jacquetta *fem* form of **James**.

Jade *fem* the name of the light-green semi-precious stone used as a first name.

Jael *fem* antelope (*Hebrew*).

Jagger *masc* a surname, meaning a carter, used as a first name (*Middle English*).

Jago *masc* a Cornish form of **James**.

Jaime *masc* a Spanish form of **James**; *fem* a variant form of **Jamie**.

Jairus *masc* he will enlighten (*Hebrew*).

Jake *masc* a diminutive form of **Jacob**, now used independently.

Jakob *masc* the German form of **Jacob, James**.

Jamal *masc fem* beauty (*Arabic*).

James *masc* a Christian form of **Jacob**; diminutive forms are **Jamie, Jem, Jim, Jimmy**.

Jamesina *fem* form of **James**; a diminutive form is **Ina**.

Jamie *masc* a diminutive form of **James**, now used independently, often as a girl's name.

Jan *masc* a diminutive form of **John**; the Dutch form of **John**; *fem* a diminutive form of **Jancis, Jane, Janet**, now used independently.

Jancis *fem* a combination of **Jan** and **Frances**; a diminutive form is **Jan**.

Jane *fem* form of **John**; variant forms are **Janet, Janeta, Janette, Janice, Janine, Jayne, Jean, Joan**; diminutive forms are **Jan, Janey, Janie**.

Janet, Janeta, Janette *fem* variant forms of **Jane**; a diminutive form is **Jan**.

Janice *fem* a variant form of **Jane**.

Janine *fem* a variant form of **Janey**.

Japheth *masc* enlargement (*Hebrew*).

Jaqueline *fem* a variant form of **Jacqueline**; a diminutive form is **Jaqui**.

Jared *masc* (servant (*Hebrew*).

Jarvis *masc* a surname form of **Gervase** used as a first name; a variant form is **Jervis**.

Jasmine, Jamsin *fem* the name of the flower used as a first name; variant forms are **Jessamine, Jessamyn, Yasmin, Yasmine**.

Jason *masc* healer (*Greek*); in Greek mythology, the hero who led the Argonauts.

Jasper *masc* treasure master (*Persian*).

Javan *masc* clay (*Hebrew*).

Javier *masc* a Portuguese and Spanish form of **Xavier**.

Jay *masc* a surname, meaning jay, the bird, used as a first name (*Old French*); *masc, fem* a diminutive form for names beginning with *J*.

Jayne *fem* a variant form of **Jane**.

Jean[1] *fem* a variant form of **Jane**; a diminutive form is **Jeanie**.

Jean[2] *masc* the French form of **John**.

Jeanette, Jeannette *fem* a diminutive form of **Jeanne**, now used independently as an English-language name.

Jeanne *fem* the French form of **Jane**; a diminutive form is **Jeanette**.

Jedidiah *masc* beloved of the Lord (*Hebrew*)—*dimin* **Jed**.

Jefferson *masc* a surname, meaning son of Jeffrey or Geffrey, used as a first name (*Old English*).

Jeffrey, Jeffery *masc* district or traveller peace (*Germanic*); a variant form is **Geoffrey**; a diminutive form is **Jeff**.

Jehudi *masc* Jewish (*Hebrew*); a variant form is **Yehudi**.

Jehuda *fem* form of **Jehudi**; a variant form is **Yehuda**.

Jem, Jemmie, Jemmy *masc dimins. of* **James**.

Jemima, Jemimah *fem* dove (*Hebrew*); diminutive forms are **Mima, Mina**.

Jemma *fem* a variant form of **Gemma**.

Jenna, Jenni, Jennie *fem* diminutive forms of **Jane, Jennifer**, now used independently; a variant form is **Jenny**.

Jennifer, Jenifer *fem* the Cornish form of **Guinevere**; diminutive forms are **Jen, Jennie, Jenny**.

Jenny *fem* a diminutive form of **Jane, Jennifer**, now used independently; a variant form is **Jennie**.

Jeremia *fem* form of **Jeremiah**.

Jeremias *masc* a Spanish form of **Jeremy**.

Jeremy, Jeremiah *masc* exalted of the Lord (*Hebrew*); a diminutive form is **Jerry**.

Jermaine *fem* a variant form of **Germaine**.

Jerome *masc* holy name (*Greek*); a diminutive form is **Jerry**.

Jérôme *masc* the French form of **Jerome**.

Jerónimo *masc* the Spanish form of **Jerome**.

Jerry *masc* a diminutive form of **Gerald, Gerard, Jeremy, Jerome**, now used independently.

Jerusha *fem* possessed; married (*Hebrew*).

Jervis *masc* a variant form of **Jarvis**.

Jess *fem* a diminutive form of **Jessica, Jessie**.

Jessamine, Jessamyn *fem* variant forms of **Jasmine**.

Jesse *masc* wealth (*Hebrew*).

Jessica *fem* God is looking (*Hebrew*); a diminutive form is **Jess**.

Jessie, Jessy *fem* diminutive forms of **Janet**, now used as names in their own right.

Jethro *masc* (*Hebrew*) superiority.

Jewel *fem* the name for a precious stone or valuable ornament used as a first name.

Jezebel *fem* domination (*Hebrew*).

Jill *fem* a diminutive form of **Gillian, Jillian**, now used independently.

Jillian *fem* form of **Julian**; diminutive forms are **Jill, Jilly**.

Jim, Jimmie, Jimmy *masc* diminutive forms of **James**.

Jo *masc* a diminutive form of **Joab, Joachim, Joseph**; *fem* a diminutive form of **Joanna, Joseph, Josepha, Josephine**.

Joab *masc* Jehovah is his Father (*Hebrew*).

Joachim *masc* God has established (*Hebrew*).

Joan, Joann, Joanna, Joanne *fem* forms of **John**; diminutive forms are **Joanie, Joni**.

Joaquin *masc* the Spanish form of **Joachim**.

Job *masc* afflicted; persecuted (*Hebrew*).

Jobina *fem* form of **Job**.

Jocelyn, Jocelin *masc, fem* little Goth (*Germanic*); diminutive forms are **Jos, Joss**.

Jock, Jockie *masc* a diminutive form of **John**.

Jodie, Jody *fem* diminutive forms of **Judith**, now used independently.

Joe, Joey *masc* diminutive forms of **Joseph**.

Joel *masc* the Lord is God (*Hebrew*).

Johan *masc* a Swedish form of **John**.

Johann *masc* a German form of **John**; a diminutive form is **Hans**.

Johanna *fem* the Latin and German form of **Jane**.

Johannes *masc* a Latin and German form of **John**.

John *masc* the gracious gift of God (*Hebrew*); diminutive forms are **Jack, Jackie, Jan, Jock, Johnnie, Johnny**.

Jolyon *masc* a variant form of **Julian**.

Jon *masc* a variant form of **John**; a diminutive form of **Jonathan**.

Jonah, Jonas *masc* dove (*Hebrew*).

Jonathan, Jonathon *masc* gift of Jehovah (*Hebrew*); a diminutive form is **Jon**.

Joni *fem* a diminutive form of **Joan**.

Jordan *masc* flowing down (*Hebrew*); diminutive forms are **Jud, Judd**.

Jordana *fem* form of **Jordan**.

Jorge *masc* the Spanish form of **George**.

Jos *masc* a diminutive form of **Joseph, Joshua**; *masc, fem* a diminutive form of **Jocelyn, Jocelin**.

Joscelin *masc, fem* a French form of **Jocelyn**.

Josceline *fem* form of **Jocelyn**.

José *masc* the Spanish form of **Joseph**; diminutive forms are **Pepe, Pepillo, Pepiro**.

Josef *masc* a German form of **Joseph**.

Josefa *fem* form of **Josef**.

Joseph *masc* God shall add (*Hebrew*); diminutive forms are **Jo, Joe, Joey, Jos**.

Josepha *fem* form of **Joseph**.

Josephine *fem* form of **Joseph**; diminutive forms are **Jo, Josie, Phenie**.

Josette *fem* a French diminutive form of **Josephine**, now used independently.

Josh *masc* a diminutive form of **Joshua**, now used independently.

Joshua *masc* God of salvation (*Hebrew*); a diminutive form is **Josh**.

Josiah, Josias *masc* given of the Lord (*Hebrew*).

Josie *fem* a diminutive form of **Josephine**.

Joss *masc, fem* a diminutive form of **Jocelyn, Jocelin, Joscelin**.

Joy *fem* the name of the feeling of intense happiness used as a first name (*English*).

Joyce *fem* sportive (*Latin*).

Juan *masc* the Spanish form of **John**, now used as an English-language form.

Juana *fem* the Spanish form of **Jane**; a diminutive form is **Juanita**.

Judah *masc* confession (*Hebrew*); a diminutive form is
Jude.

Jud, Judd *masc* diminutive forms of **Jordan**, also used
independently.

Jude *masc* a diminutive form of **Judah**.

Judie, Judi *fem* diminutive forms of **Judith**, now used
independently.

Judith *fem* praised (*Hebrew*); diminutive forms are
Jodie, Judy.

Judy *fem* a diminutive form of **Judith**, now used independently.

Jules *masc* the French form of **Julius**; a diminutive form
of **Julian, Julius**; *fem* a diminutive form of **Julia, Juliana**.

Julia *fem* forms of **Julius**; a variant form is **Juliana**; a
diminutive form is **Julie**.

Julian *masc* sprung from or belonging to Julius (*Latin*);
a variant form is **Jolyon**.

Juliana *fem* form of **Julius**.

Julie, Juliet *fem* diminutive forms of **Julia**, now used
independently.

Julien *masc* the French form of **Julian**.

Julienne *fem* form of **Julien**.

Julieta *fem* a Spanish form of **Julia**.

Juliette *fem* the French form of **Julia**, now used as an
English-language form.

Julio *masc* a Spanish form of **Julius**.

Julius *masc* soft-haired (*Greek*).

June *fem* the name of the month used as a first name (*Latin*).

Juno *fem* queen of heaven, in Roman mythology the equivalent of **Hera** (*Latin*).

Justin *masc* the English form of *Justinus*, a Roman family name from **Justus** (*Latin*); a variant form is **Justinian**.

Justina, Justine *fem* forms of **Justin**.

Justinian, Justus *masc* variant forms of **Justin**.

Justus *masc* fair, just (*Latin*).

K

Kalantha, Kalanthe *fem* variant forms of **Calantha**.

Kalypso *fem* a variant form of **Calypso**.

Kane *masc* a surname, meaning warrior, used as a first name (*Irish Gaelic*).

Kara *fem* a variant form of **Cara**.

Karel *masc* the Czech and Dutch form of **Charles**.

Karen *fem* a Dutch and Scandinavian form of **Katherine**.

Karin *fem* a Scandinavian form of **Katherine**.

Karl *masc* a German form of **Charles**.

Karla *fem* form of **Karl**.

Karlotte *fem* a German form of **Charlotte**.

Karol *masc* the Polish form of **Charles**.

Karoline *fem* a German form of **Caroline**.

Karr *masc* a variant form of **Kerr**.

Kasimir *masc* peace (*Polish*).

Kaspar *masc* the German form of **Jasper**.

Kate *fem* a diminutive form of **Katherine**, also used independently.

Katerina *fem* a variant form of **Katherine**.

Kath, Kathie, Kathy *fem* diminutive forms of **Katherine**.

Katharina, Katharine *fem* German forms of **Katherine**; a diminutive form is **Katrine**.

Katherine *fem* pure (*Greek*); diminutive forms are **Kate, Kath, Katie, Katy, Kay, Kit, Kittie**.

Kathleen *fem* an Irish form of **Katherine**.

Kathryn *fem* an American form of **Katherine**.

Katie *fem* a diminutive form of **Katherine**, now used independently.

Katinka *fem* a Russian form of **Katherine**.

Katrine *fem* a diminutive form of **Katharina**; a variant form of **Katriona**; the name of a Scottish loch, meaning wood of Eriu, used as a first name.

Katriona *fem* a variant form of **Catriona**; a variant form is **Katrine**.

Katy *fem* a diminutive form of **Katherine**, now used independently.

Kavan *masc* a variant form of **Cavan**.

Kay *masc* giant (*Scots Gaelic*); *fem* a diminutive form of **Katherine**, now used independently; a variant form is **Kaye**.

Kayla, Kayleigh, Kayley *fem* derivation uncertain, possibly slender (*Irish Gaelic*), a combination of **Kay** and **Leigh**, or a variant form of **Kelly**.

Kean, Keane *masc* anglicized forms of **Cian**.

Kedar *masc* powerful (*Arabic*).

Keefe *masc* noble, admirable (*Irish Gaelic*).

Keegan *masc* a surname, meaning son of Egan, used as a first name (*Irish Gaelic*).

Keenan *masc* a surname, meaning little ancient one, used as a first name (*Irish Gaelic*).

Keir *masc* a surname, meaning swarthy, used as a first name (*Scots Gaelic*).

Keira *fem* a variant spelling of **Ciara**.

Keith *masc* a placename and surname, meaning wood, used as a first name (*Celtic*).

Keld *masc* a Danish form of **Keith**.

Kelly *fem* a surname, meaning descendant of war, used as a first name (*Irish Gaelic*).

Kelsey *masc* a surname, meaning victory, used as a first name (*Old English*).

Kelvin *masc* the name of a Scottish river, meaning narrow water, used as a first name (*Scots Gaelic*).

Kemp *masc* a surname, meaning warrior (*Old English*) or athlete (*Middle English*), used as a first name.

Ken *masc* a diminutive form of **Kendall, Kendrick, Kenelm, Kennard, Kennedy, Kenneth**.

Kendall, Kendal, Kendell *masc* a surname, meaning valley of the holy river, used as a first name (*Celtic/Old English*); a diminutive form is **Ken**.

Kendra *fem* form of **Kendrick**.

Kendrick *masc* a surname, meaning hero, used as a first name (*Welsh*); a variant form is **Kenrick**; a diminutive form is **Ken**.

Kenelm *masc* a defender of his kindred (*Old English*); a diminutive form is **Ken**.

Kennard *masc* a surname, meaning strong and vigorous, or cow yard, used as a first name (*Old English*); a diminutive form is **Ken**.

Kennedy *masc* a surname, meaning helmeted or ugly head, used as a first name (*Gaelic*); a diminutive form is **Ken**.

Kennet *masc* a Scandinavian form of Kenneth; diminutive forms are **Ken**, **Kent**.

Kenneth *masc* fire-born; handsome (*Gaelic*); diminutive forms are **Ken**, **Kennie**, **Kenny**.

Kennie, Kenny *masc* diminutive forms of **Kenneth** and other names beginning with Ken-.

Kenrick *masc* a variant form of **Kendrick**.

Kent *masc* a surname, meaning from the county of Kent (meaning border), used as a first name (*Celtic*); a diminutive form of **Kennet**, **Kenton**.

Kenton *masc* a surname, meaning settlement on the river Kenn, or royal place, used as a first name (*Old English*); diminutive forms are **Ken**, **Kent**.

Kenyon *masc* white-haired (*Gaelic*); a surname, meaning mound of Ennion, used as a first name (*Welsh*).

Kermit *masc* son of Diarmid (*Irish Gaelic*).

Kern *masc* dark one (*Gaelic*).

Kerr *masc* a Scottish form of the surname **Carr**, used as a first name; a variant form is **Karr**.

Kerry *fem, masc* the name of the Irish county used as a first name.

Kester *masc* a diminutive form of **Christopher**.

Keturah *fem* incense (*Hebrew*).

Kevin

Kevin, Kevan *masc* comely, loved (*Irish Gaelic*); a diminutive form is **Kev**.

Kezia, Keziah *fem* the cassia tree (*Hebrew*); diminutive forms are **Kizzie, Kizzy**.

Kieran *masc* an anglicized form of **Ciaran**.

Kiernan *masc* a variant form of **Tiernan**.

Kim *fem* a diminutive form of **Kimberley**, also used independently.

Kimberley *fem* a surname, meaning wood clearing, used as a first name (*Old English*); a diminutive form is **Kim**.

King *masc* the title of a monarch or a surname, meaning appearance, or serving in a royal household, used as a first name (*Old English*); a diminutive form of names beginning with King-.

Kingsley *masc* a surname, meaning king's meadow, used as a first name (*Old English*).

Kingston *masc* a placename and surname, meaning king's farm, used as a first name (*Old English*).

Kinsey *masc* a surname, meaning royal victor, used as a first name (*Old English*).

Kirby *masc* a surname, meaning church village or farm, used as a first name (*Old Norse*).

Kirk *masc* a surname, meaning one who lives near a church, used as a first name (*Old Norse*).

Kirkwood *masc* a surname, meaning church wood, used as a first name (*Old Norse/Old English*).

Kirsten *fem* a Scandinavian form of **Christine**.

Kirstie, Kirsty *fem* a diminutive form of **Kirstin**, now used independently.

Kirstin *fem* a Scots form of **Christine**; a diminutive form is **Kirstie.**

Kish *masc* a gift (*Hebrew*).

Kit *masc* a diminutive form of **Christopher, Kristopher**; *fem* a diminutive form of **Katherine**.

Kittie, Kitty *fem* diminutive forms of **Katherine**.

Kizzie, Kizzy *fem* diminutive forms of **Kezia**.

Klara *fem* the German form of **Clara**.

Klaus *masc* a variant form of **Claus**.

Klemens *masc* a German form of **Clement**.

Knight *masc* a surname, meaning bound to serve a feudal lord as a mounted soldier, used as a first name (*Old English*).

Knut *masc* a variant form of **Canute**.

Konrad *masc* a German and Swedish form of **Conrad**.

Konstanz *masc* the German form of **Constant**.

Konstanze *fem* the German form of **Constance**.

Kora *fem* a variant form of **Cora**.

Korah *masc* baldness (*Hebrew*).

Kris *masc* a diminutive form of **Kristoffer, Kristopher**.

Kristeen *fem* a variant form of **Christine**.

Kirstel *fem* a German form of **Christine**.

Kristen *masc* the Danish form of **Christian**, now also used in English as a girl's name.

Kristian *masc* a Swedish form of **Christian**.

Kristina *fem* the Swedish form of **Christina**.

Kristoffer

Kristoffer *masc* a Scandinavian form of **Christopher**.

Kristopher *masc* a variant form of **Christopher**; diminutive forms are **Kit, Kris**.

Kurt *masc* a diminutive form of **Conrad**, now used independently; a variant form is **Curt**.

Kyle *masc* narrow (*Scots Gaelic*); the name of a region of southwest Scotland used as a surname.

Kylie *fem* a combination of **Kyle** and **Kelly**.

Kyrena *fem* a variant form of **Cyrena**.

L

Laban *masc* white (*Hebrew*).

Lachlan *masc* from the land of lakes (*Scots Gaelic*).

Lacey *masc, fem* a surname, meaning from Lassy in the Calvados region of Normandy, used as a first name (Old French).

Ladislao *masc* an Italian form of **Laszlo**.

Ladislas *masc* rule of glory (*Polish/Latin*).

Laszlo *masc* the Hungarian form of **Ladislas**.

Laetitia *fem* happiness (*Latin*); variant forms are **Latisha, Letitia**.

Laing *masc* a variant form of **Lang**.

Laird *masc* a Scots form of the surname Lord, meaning master, landowner (*Old English*), used as a first name.

Lalage *fem* chattering (*Greek-Latin*); a diminutive form is **Lallie, Lally**.

Lambert *masc* illustrious with landed possessions (*Germanic*).

Lamberto *masc* the Italian form of **Lambert**.

Lamond, Lamont *masc* a surname, meaning law giver, used as a first name (*Old Norse/Scots Gaelic*).

Lana *fem* a variant form of **Alana**.

Lance *masc* land (*Germanic*); a diminutive form of **Lancelot**.

Lancelot *masc* a little lance or warrior; or a servant (*French*); a diminutive form is **Lance**.

Lander, Landor *masc* variant forms of the surname **Lavender**.

Lane *masc* a surname, meaning narrow road, lane, used as a first name (*Old English*).

Lang *masc* a Scottish form of the surname Long, meaning tall or long, used as a first name (*Old English*); a variant form is **Laing**.

Langford *masc* a surname, meaning long ford, used as a first name (*Old English*).

Langley *masc* a surname, meaning long meadow, used as a first name (*Old English*).

Lara *fem* a diminutive form of **Larissa** (*Latin*).

Laraine *fem* a variant form of **Lorraine**; the queen (*Old French*).

Larissa, Larisa *fem* meaning uncertain, possibly happy as a lark (*Greek/Russian*); diminutve forms are **Lara**, **Lissa**.

Lark *fem* the English word for a bird famed for rising early and for its song used as a first name.

Larry *masc* a diminutive form of **Laurence, Lawrence**.

Lars *masc* a Scandinavian form of **Laurence**.

Larsen, Larson *masc* son of Lars (*Scandinavian*).

Lascelles *masc* a surname, meaning hermitage or cell, used as a first name (*Old French*).

Latham, Lathom *masc* a surname, meaning barns, used as a first name (*Old Norse*).

Latimer *masc* a surname, meaning interpreter, used as a first name (*Old French*).

Latisha *fem* a variant form of **Laetitia**.

Laura *fem* laurel, bay tree (*Latin*); a diminutive form is **Laurie**.

Laurabel *fem* a combination of **Laura** and **Mabel**.

Laurel *fem* a name for the evergreen bay tree used as a first name.

Lauren *fem* form of **Laurence**; a variant form is **Loren**; a diminutive form is **Laurie**.

Laurence *masc* from Laurentium in Italy, place of laurels (*Latin*); a variant form is **Lawrence**; diminutive forms are **Larry, Laurie**.

Laurens *masc* a Dutch form of **Lawrence**.

Laurent *masc* the French form of **Laurence**.

Laurette *fem* a French form of **Laura**; a variant form is **Lauretta**.

Laurie *masc* a diminutive form of **Laurence**; a surname form of this used as a first name; variant forms are **Lawrie, Lawry**; *fem* a dimuntive form of **Laura, Lauren**.

Lavender *fem* the English name of the plant that bears blue or mauve flowers used as a first name; *masc* a surname, meaning launderer, used as a first name (*Old French*); a variant form is **Lander**.

Laverne *fem* the alder tree (*Old French*); diminutive forms are **Verna, Verne**.

Lavinia, Lavina *fem* of Latium in Italy (*Latin*).

Lawrence *masc* a variant form of of **Laurence**; diminutive forms are **Larry, Lawrie, Lawry**.

Lawrie, Lawry *masc* diminutive forms of **Lawrence**; a variant form of **Laurie**.

Lawson *masc* a surname, meaning son of Lawrence, used as a first name (*Old English*).

Lawton *masc* a surname, meaning from the place on the hill, used as a first name (*Old English*).

Layton *masc* a variant form of **Leighton**.

Lazarus *masc* destitute of help (*Hebrew*).

Lea *fem* a variant form of **Leah, Lee**.

Leah *fem* a cow, denoting domestic ability or value (*Hebrew*); variant forms are **Lea, Lee**.

Leal, Leale *masc* a surname, meaning loyal, true, used as a first name (*Old French*).

Leander *masc* lion man (*Greek*).

Leane *fem* a variant form of **Leanne, Liane**.

Leandre *masc* a French form of **Leander**.

Leandro *masc* an Italian form of **Leander**.

Leanne *fem* a combination of **Lee** and **Anne**; a variant form is **Leane**.

Leanora, Leanore *fem* German variant forms of **Eleanor**.

Leda *fem* mother of beauty; in Greek mythology, a queen of Sparta who was visited by Zeus (who appeared to her in the form of a swan) and gave birth to Helen (*Greek*).

Lee *masc fem* a surname, meaning field or meadow, used as a first name (*Old English*); a variant form is **Leigh**; *fem* a variant form of **Leah**.

Leif *masc* beloved one (*Old Norse*).

Leigh *masc* a variant form of **Lee**.

Leighton *masc* a surname, meaning herb garden, used as a first name (*Old English*); a variant form is **Layton**.

Leila *fem* night, dark (*Arabic*); variant forms are **Lela, Lila, Lilah**.

Leith *masc* a placename, meaning moist place (*Celtic*) or grey (*Scots Gaelic*), used as a first name.

Lela *fem* a variant form of **Leila**.

Leland *masc* a variant form of **Leyland**.

Lemuel *masc* created by God (*Hebrew*); a diminutive form is **Lem**.

Len *masc* a diminutive form of **Leonard, Lennox, Lionel**.

Lena *fem* a diminutive form of **Helena**, etc, also used independently.

Lennard *masc* a variant form of **Leonard**.

Lennie *masc* a diminutive form of **Leonard, Lennox, Lionel**.

Lennox *masc* a placename and surname, meaning abounding in elm trees, used as a first name (*Scots Gaelic*).

Lenny *masc* a diminutive form of **Leonard, Lennox, Lionel**; a variant form is **Lonnie**.

Lenora *fem* a variant form of **Leonora**.

Leo *masc* lion (*Latin*); a variant form is **Leon**.

Leon *masc* a variant form of **Leo**.

Leona *fem* a variant form of **Leonie**.

Leonard *masc* strong or brave as a lion (*Germanic*); a variant form is **Lennard**; diminutive forms are **Len, Lennie, Lenny**.

Leonarda *fem* form of **Leonard**.

Leonardo *masc* an Italian form of **Leonard**.

Leonhard *masc* a German form of **Leonard**.

Leonidas *masc* lion-like (*Greek*).

Leonie *fem* form of **Leo, Leon**; a variant form is **Leona**.

Leonora *fem* an Italian form of **Eleanor**; a variant form is **Lenora**; a diminutive form is **Nora**.

Leontine, Leontina *fem* form of **Leontius**.

Leontius *masc* of the lion (*Latin*).

Leontyne *fem* a variant form of Leontine.

Leopold *masc* bold for the people (*Germanic*).

Leopoldina, Leopoldine *fem* forms of Leopold.

Leopoldo *masc* an Italian and Spanish form of **Leopold**.

Leroy *masc* the king (*Old French*); a variant form is **Elroy**; diminutive forms are **Lee, Roy**.

Leslie *masc, fem* a surname, meaning garden by water, used as a first name (*Gaelic*).

Lesley *fem* form of Leslie.

Lester *masc* a surname, meaning from the Roman site

(i.e. the present city of Leicester), used as a first name (*Old English*).

Leticia, Letitia *fem* variant forms of **Laetitia**.

Letizia *fem* an Italian form of **Laetitia**.

Lettice *fem* a variant form of **Laetitia**; diminutive forms are **Lettie, Letty**.

Lev *masc* a Russian form of **Leo**.

Levi *masc* adhesion (*Hebrew*).

Lewis *masc* bold warrior (*Germanic*); diminutive forms are **Lew, Lewie**.

Lex *masc* a diminutive form of **Alexander**.

Lexie, Lexy *fem* diminutive forms of **Alexandra**.

Leyland *masc* a surname, meaning fallow or untilled land, used as a first name (*Old English*); a variant form is **Leland**.

Liam *masc* the Irish form of **William**.

Liana, Liane, Lianna, Lianne *fem* sun (*Greek*); variant forms are **Leane, Leana, Leanna**.

Libby *fem* a diminutive form of **Elizabeth**.

Lidia *fem* an Italian and Spanish form of **Lydia**.

Liese *fem* a diminutive form of **Elisabeth**, now used independently.

Lil *fem* a diminutive form of **Lilian, Lily**.

Lila *fem* a variant form of **Leila**; a diminutive form of **Delilah**.

Lilac *fem* bluish (*Persian*), the English name of the syringa plant with fragrant purple or white flowers used as a first name.

Lilah *fem* a variant form of **Leila**; a diminutive form of **Delilah**.

Lili *fem* a variant form of **Lilie**.

Lilian *fem* a diminutive form of **Elizabeth**; a variant form of **Lily**; a variant form is **Lillian**.

Lilias, Lillias *fem* Scottish forms of **Lilian**.

Lilibet *fem* a diminutive form of **Elizabeth**.

Lilie *fem* a German form of **Lily**; a variant form is **Lili**.

Lilith *fem* of the night (*Hebrew*).

Lilli *fem* a variant form of **Lily**.

Lillian *fem* a variant form of **Lilian**.

Lily *fem* the name of the flowering plant with showy blossoms used as a first name; a variant form is **Lilli**; a diminutive form is **Lil**.

Lin *fem* a diminutive form of **Linda**.

Lina *fem* a diminutive form of **Selina** and names ending in -lina, -line.

Lincoln *masc* a placename and surname, meaning the place by the pool, used as a first name (*Celtic/Latin*).

Linda *fem* a diminutive form of **Belinda, Rosalind**, etc, now used independently; a variant form is **Lynda**; diminutive forms are **Lin, Lindie, Lindy**.

Lindall, Lindell *masc* a surname, meaning valley of lime trees, used as a first name (*Old English*).

Lindie *fem* a diminutive form of **Linda**.

Lindley *masc* a placename and surname, meaning lime tree meadow or flax field, used as a first name (*Old English*); a variant form is **Linley**.

Lindsay, Lindsey *masc, fem* a surname, meaning island of Lincoln, used as a first name; variant forms are **Linsay, Linsey, Linzi, Lynsay, Lynsey**.

Lindy *fem* a diminutive form of **Linda**.

Linford *masc* a surname, meaning from the ford of the lime tree or flax field, used as a first name (*Old English*).

Linley *masc* a variant form of **Lindley**.

Linnette *fem* a variant form of **Lynette**.

Linsay, Linsey *masc, fem* variant forms of **Lindsay**.

Linton *masc* a surname, meaning flax place, used as a first name (*Old English*).

Linus *masc* flaxen-haired (*Greek*).

Linzi *fem* a variant form of **Lindsay**.

Lionel *masc* young lion (*Latin*); a diminutive form is **Len**.

Lis *fem* a diminutive form of **Elisabeth**.

Lisa *fem* a diminutive form of **Elizabeth**, now used independently; a variant form is **Liza**.

Lisbeth *fem* a diminutive form of **Elisabeth**.

Lisette *fem* a diminutive form of **Louise**.

Lisle *masc* a surname, meaning island, or from Lisle in Normandy, used as a first name (*Old French*); variant forms are **Lyall, Lyle**.

Lissa *fem* a diminutive form of **Larissa, Melissa**.

Lister *masc* a surname, meaning dyer, used as a first name (*Old English*).

Litton *masc* a placename and surname, meaning loud

torrent, used as a first name (*Old English*); a variant form is **Lytton**.

Livia *fem* a variant form of **Olivia**.

Liz *fem* a diminutive form of **Elizabeth**.

Liza *fem* a variant form of **Lisa**.

Lizbeth *fem* a diminutive form of **Elizabeth**.

Lizzie, Lizzy *fem* diminutive forms of **Elizabeth**.

Llewelyn *masc* leader, ruler (*Welsh*).

Lloyd *masc* a surname, meaning grey, used as a first name (*Welsh*).

Locke *masc* a surname, meaning enclosure, stronghold, used as a first name (*Old English*).

Logan *masc* a surname, meaning little hollow, used as a first name (*Scots Gaelic*).

Lois *fem* meaning uncertain, possibly good, desirable (*Greek*).

Lola *fem* a diminutive form of **Dolores, Carlotta**, now used independently.

Lombard *masc* a surname, meaning long beard, used as a first name (*Germanic*).

Lona *fem* a diminutive form of **Maelona**.

Lonnie *masc* a variant form of **Lenny**; a diminutive form of **Alonso**.

Lora *fem* a Welsh form of **Laura**.

Lorcan, Lorcán *masc* fierce (*Irish Gaelic*).

Lorelei *fem* the name of a rock in the River Rhine from where in German legend a siren lured boatmen.

Loren *fem* a variant form of **Lauren**.

Lorenz *masc* the German form of **Laurence**.

Lorenzo *masc* the Italian and Spanish form of **Laurence**.

Loretta *fem* a variant form of **Lauretta**.

Loring *masc* a surname, meaning man from Lorraine (bold and famous), used as a first name (*Germanic/ Old French*).

Lorn *masc* a variant form of **Lorne**.

Lorna *fem* a name invented by R. D. Blackmore, possibly from **Lorne**, for the heroine of his novel *Lorna Doone*.

Lorne *masc* a Scottish placename (the northern area of Argyll), of uncertain meaning, used as a first name; a variant form is **Lorn**.

Lorraine *fem* a surname meaning man from Lorraine (bold and famous) used as a first name (*Old French*); a variant form is **Laraine**.

Lot *masc* a veil; a covering (*Hebrew*).

Lotario *masc* the Italian form of **Luther**.

Lothaire *masc* the French form of **Luther**.

Lottie, Lotty *fem* diminutive forms of **Charlotte**.

Lotus *fem* the English name of a fruit that in Greek mythology was said to induce langour and forgetfulness.

Lou *masc* a diminutive form of **Louis**; *fem* a diminutive form of **Louisa, Louise**.

Louella *fem* a combination of **Louise** and **Ella**.

Louis *masc* the French form of **Lewis**; diminutive forms are **Lou, Louie**.

Louisa *fem* form of **Louis**.

Louise *fem* the French form of **Louisa**, now used widely as an English-language form; diminutive forms are **Lisette, Lou**.

Lovel, Lovell *masc* a surname, meaning little wolf, used as a first name (*Old French*); a variant form is **Lowell**.

Lowell *masc* a variant form of **Lovel**.

Luc *masc* the French form of **Luke**.

Luca *masc* the Italian form of **Luke**.

Lucan *masc* a placename, meaning place of elms, used as a first name (*Irish Gaelic*).

Lucas *masc* a variant form of **Luke**.

Luce *fem* a diminutive form of **Lucy**.

Lucia *fem* form of **Lucian**.

Lucian *masc* belonging to or sprung from Lucius (*Latin*).

Lucien *masc* a French form of **Lucian**.

Luciano *masc* an Italian form of **Lucian**.

Lucienne *fem* form of **Lucien**.

Lucifer *masc* light bringer (*Latin*).

Lucilla *fem* a diminutive form of **Lucia**.

Lucille, Lucile *fem* French forms of **Lucia**, now used as English-language forms.

Lucinda *fem* a variant form of **Lucia**; a diminutive form is **Cindy**.

Lucio *masc* a Spanish form of **Luke**.

Lucius *masc* born at break of day (*Latin*).

Lucrèce *fem* a French form of **Lucretia**.

Lucretia, Lucrece *fem* gain; light (*Latin*).

Lucretius *masc* form of **Lucretia**.

Lucrezia *fem* an Italian form of **Lucretia**.

Lucy *fem* a popular form of **Lucia**; a diminutive form is **Luce**.

Ludlow *masc* a placename, meaning hill by the rapid river, used as a first name (*Old English*).

Ludmila, Ludmilla *fem* of the people (*Russian*).

Ludovic, Ludovick *masc* variant forms of of **Lewis**; a diminutive form is **Ludo**.

Ludvig *masc* a Swedish form of **Lewis**.

Ludwig *masc* the German form of **Lewis**.

Luella *fem* a variant form of **Louella**.

Luigi *masc* an Italian form of **Lewis**.

Luis *masc* a Spanish form of **Lewis**.

Luisa *fem* an Italian and Spanish form of **Louisa**.

Luise *fem* the German form of **Louisa**; a diminutive form is **Lulu**.

Lukas *masc* a Swedish form of **Luke, Lucas**.

Luke *masc* of Lucania in Italy (*Latin*).

Lulu *fem* a diminutive form of **Luise**.

Lundy *masc* a placename, meaning puffin island, used as a first name (Old Norse); born on Monday (*Old French*).

Lutero *masc* a Spanish form of **Luther**.

Luther *masc* illustrious warrior (*Germanic*).

Lyall *masc* a variant form of **Lisle**.

Lycurgus *masc* wolf driver (*Greek*).

Lydia *fem* a native of Lydia in Asia Minor (*Greek*).

Lyle *masc* a variant form of **Lisle**.

Lyn *fem* a diminutive form of **Lynette, Lynsay**.

Lynda *fem* a variant form of **Linda**; diminutive forms are **Lyn, Lynn, Lynne**.

Lynden, Lyndon *masc* a surname, meaning dweller by lime trees, used as a first name; a diminutive form is **Lyn**.

Lynette *fem* an English form of **Eluned**; variant forms are **Lynnette, Linnette**.

Lynn *fem* a diminutive form of **Lynda**, now used independently.

Lynn *masc* a surname, meaning pool or waterfall, used as a first name (*Celtic*); diminutive forms are **Lyn, Lin, Linn**.

Lynnette *fem* a variant form of **Lynette**.

Lynsay, Lynsey *masc, fem* variant forms of **Lindsay**.

Lyris *fem* She who plays the harp (*Greek*).

Lysander *masc* liberator (*Greek*); a diminutive form is **Sandy**.

Lysandra *fem* form of **Lysander**.

Lyss *masc* a diminutive form of **Ulysses**.

Lytton *masc* a variant form of **Litton**.

M

Maarten *masc* a Dutch form of **Martin**.

Mabel *fem* diminutive forms of **Amabel**, also used independently; a variant form is **Maybelle**.

Mabelle *fem* a French form of **Mabel**.

Madalena *fem* the Spanish form of **Madeleine**.

Maddalena *fem* the Italian form of **Madeleine**.

Maddie, Maddy *fem* diminutive forms of **Madeleine**.

Madeleine, Madeline *fem* from Magdala on the Sea of Galilee (*French*); a variant form is **Magdalene**; diminutive forms are **Maddie, Maddy, Mala**.

Madge *fem* diminutive forms of **Margaret, Marjory**.

Madison *masc* a surname, meaning son of Matthew or Maud, used as a first name (*Old English*).

Madoc *masc* good; beneficent (*Welsh*).

Madonna *fem* my lady, a title of the Virgin Mary (*Italian*).

Mae *fem* a variant form of **May**.

Maelona *fem* princess (*Welsh*); a diminutive form is **Lona**.

Maeve *fem* intoxicating (*Celtic*); variant forms are **Mave, Meave**.

Magda *fem* a German and Scandinavian form of
Magdalene.

Magdalene, Magdalen *fem* variant forms of **Madeleine**.

Magee *masc* a surname, meaning son of Hugh, used a a
first name (*Irish Gaelic*); a variant form is **McGee**.

Maggie *fem* diminutive forms of **Margaret**.

Magnolia *fem* the name of a tree with showy flowers,
named after the French botanist Pierre Magnol, used
as a first name.

Magnus *masc* great (*Latin*).

Mahalia *fem* tenderness (*Hebrew*).

Mai, Mair *fem* Welsh forms of **May**.

Maida *fem* the name of a place in Calabria in Spain,
where a battle was fought in 1806, used as a first name;
a diminutive form is **Maidie**.

Mairead *fem* an Irish form of **Margaret**.

Mairi *fem* Scots Gaelic form of **Mary**.

Maisie *fem* diminutive forms of **Margaret**, also used independently.

Maitland *masc* a surname, meaning unproductive land,
used as a first name (*Old French*).

Makepeace *masc* a surname, meaning peacemaker, used
as a first name (*Old English*).

Mala *fem* a diminutive form of **Madeleine**.

Malachi *masc* messenger of the Lord (*Hebrew*).

Malcolm *masc* servant of Columba (*Scots Gaelic*); diminutive forms are **Calum, Mal**.

Malise *masc* servant of Jesus (*Scots Gaelic*).

Mallory *masc* a surname, meaning unfortunate, luckless, used as a first name (*Old French*).

Malone *masc* a surname, meaning follower of St John, used as a first name (*Irish Gaelic*).

Malvina *fem* smooth brow (*Scots Gaelic*).

Mame, Mamie *fem* diminutive forms of **Mary**, now used independently.

Manasseh *masc* forgetfulness (*Hebrew*).

Manda *fem* a diminutive form of **Amanda**.

Mandy *fem* diminutive forms of **Amanda, Miranda**, now used independently; *masc* little man (*German*).

Manette *fem* a French form of **Mary**.

Manfred *masc* man of peace (*Germanic*); a diminutive form is **Manny**.

Manfredi *masc* the Italian form of **Manfred**.

Manfried *masc* a German form of **Manfred**.

Manley *masc* a surname, meaning brave, upright, used as a first name (*Middle English*).

Manny *masc* diminutive forms of **Emmnauel, Immanuel, Manfred**.

Manuel *masc* the Spanish form of **Emmanuel**.

Manuela *fem* God with us (*Spanish*).

Marc *masc* a French form of **Mark**; a variant form of **Marcus**.

Marcel *masc* a French form of **Marcellus**.

Marcela *fem* a Spanish form of **Marcella**.

Marcella *fem* form of **Marcellus**.

Marcelle *fem* a French form of **Marcella**.

Marcello *masc* the Italian form of **Marcel**.

Marcellus *masc* the Latin and Scots Gaelic form of **Mark**.

Marcelo *masc* a Spanish form of **Marcel**.

Marcia *fem* form of **Marcius**; a variant form is **Marsha**; diminutive forms are **Marcie, Marcy**.

Marcius *masc* a variant form of **Mark**.

Marco *masc* the Italian form of **Mark**.

Marcos *masc* the Spanish form of **Mark**.

Marcus *masc* the Latin form of **Mark**, now used as an English variant form; a variant form is **Marc**.

Mared *fem* a Welsh form of **Margaret**.

Margaret *fem* a pearl (*Greek*); diminutive forms are **Greta, Madge, Maggie, Margie, May, Meg, Meggie, Meta, Peg**.

Margarete *fem* the Danish and German form of **Margaret**; diminutive forms are **Grete, Gretchen**.

Margaretha *fem* a Dutch form of **Margaret**.

Margarita *fem* the Spanish form of **Margaret**; a diminutive form is **Rita**.

Margaux *fem* a variant form of **Margot**.

Margery *fem* in the Middle Ages a diminutive form of **Margaret**, but now a name in its own right; a variant form is **Marjorie**; a diminutive form is **Madge, Marge**.

Margherita *fem* the Italian form of **Margaret**; a diminutive form is **Rita**.

Margie *fem* diminutive form of **Margaret**.

Margo, Margot *fem* diminutive forms of **Margaret, Marguerite**, now used independently; a variant form is **Margaux**.

Marguerite *fem* the French form of **Margaret**; diminutive forms are **Margo, Margot**.

Mari *fem* an Irish and Welsh form of **Mary**.

Maria *fem* the Latin, Italian, German, and Spanish forms of **Mary**; a diminutive form is **Ria**.

Mariam *fem* the Greek form of **Mary**.

Marian *fem* a French form of **Marion**.

Marianna *fem* an Italian form of **Marianne, Marion**.

Marianne *fem* a French and German form of **Marion**; a compound of **Mary** and **Ann**.

Maribella *fem* a compound of **Mary** and **Bella**.

Marie *fem* a French form of **Mary**; a diminutive form is **Marion**.

Marietta *fem* diminutive form of **Maria**, also used independently

Marigold *fem* the name of the golden flower used as a first name.

Marilyn *fem* diminutive form of **Mary**, also used independently.

Marina *fem* of the sea (*Latin*).

Mario *masc* an Italian form of **Marius**.

Marion *fem* a variant form of **Mary**; *masc* a French form of **Mary**, in compliment to the Virgin Mary.

Marisa *fem* summit (*Hebrew*).

Marius *masc* martial (*Latin*).

Marjorie, Marjory *fem* variant forms of **Margery**.

Mark *masc* a hammer; a male; sprung from Mars (*Latin*); a variant form is **Marcus**.

Markus *masc* the German and Sweidsh form of **Mark**.

Marland *masc* a surname, meaning lake land, used as a first name (*Old English*).

Marlene *fem* a contraction of **Maria Magdalena** (*German*).

Marlo *masc* a variant form of **Marlow**.

Marlon *masc* of uncertain meaning, possibly hawk-like (*French*).

Marlow *masc* a placename and surname, meaning land of the former pool, used as a first name (*Old English*); variant forms are **Marlo, Marlowe**.

Marmaduke *masc* a mighty noble; Madoc's servant (*Celtic*); a diminutive form is **Duke**.

Marmion *masc* a surname, meaning brat, monkey, used as a first name (*Old French*).

Marsden *masc* a surname, meaning boundary valley, used as a first name (*Old English*).

Marsh *masc* a surname, meaning marsh, used as a first name (*Old English*).

Marsha *fem* a variant form of **Marcia**.

Marshall *masc* a surname, meaning horse servant, used as a first name (*Germanic*).

Marston *masc* a surname, meaning place by a marsh, used as a first name (*Old English*).

Marta *fem* the Italian, Spanish and Swedish form of

Martha, now used as an English-language form; a variant form is **Martita**.

Martha *fem* the ruler of the house; sorrowful (*Hebrew*); diminutive forms are **Mat, Mattie**.

Marthe *fem* the French and German form of **Martha**.

Marti *fem* a diminutive form of **Martina, Martine**.

Martijn *masc* a Dutch form of **Martin**.

Martin *masc* of Mars; warlike (*Latin*); a variant form is **Martyn**; a diminutive form is **Marty**.

Martina *fem* forms of **Martin**; a diminutive form is **Marti**.

Martine *fem* the French form of **Martina**, now used as an English-language form; a diminutive form is **Marti**.

Martino *masc* an Italian and Spanish form of **Martin**.

Martita *fem* a variant form of **Marta**; a diminutive form is **Tita**.

Marty *masc* a diminutive form of **Martin**.

Martyn *masc* a variant form of **Martin**.

Marvin *masc* a variant form of **Mervin**.

Marwood *masc* a surname, meaning bigger or boundary wood, used as a first name (*Old English*).

Mary *fem* bitter; their rebellion; star of the sea (*Hebrew*); variant forms are **Marion, Miriam**; diminutive forms are **Mamie, May, Minnie, Mollie, Polly**.

Maryann, Maryanne *fem* compounds of **Mary** and **Ann** or **Anne**.

Marylou *fem* a compound of **Mary** and **Louise**.

Massimiliano *masc* the Italian form of **Maximilian**.

Mat

Mat *masc* a diminutive form of **Matthew**; *fem* a diminutive form of **Martha, Mathilda**.

Mateo *masc* the Spanish form of **Matthew**.

Mather *masc* a surname, meaning mower, used as a first name (*Old English*).

Matheson, Mathieson *masc* a surname, meaning son of Matthew, used as a first name.

Mathias *masc* a variant form of **Matthias**.

Mathieu *masc* a French form of **Matthew**.

Mathilda *fem* a variant form of **Matilda**.

Mathilde *fem* the French form of **Matilda**.

Matilda *fem* mighty battle maid; heroine (*Germanic*); a variant form is **Mathilda**; diminutive forms are **Mat, Mattie, Tilda, Tilly**.

Matilde *fem* the Italian and Spanish form of **Matilda**.

Matt *masc* a diminutive form of **Matthew**.

Mattaeus *masc* a Danish form of **Matthew**.

Matteo *masc* the Italian form of **Matthew**.

Matthais *masc* a Greek form of **Matthew**.

Matthäus *masc* a German form of **Matthew**.

Mattheus *masc* a Dutch and Swedish form of **Matthew**.

Matthew *masc* gift of Jehovah (*Hebrew*); diminutive forms are **Mat, Matt, Mattie**.

Matthias *masc* a Latin form of **Matthew**; a variant form is **Mathias**.

Matthieu *masc* the French form of **Matthew**.

Mattie *fem* a diminutive form of **Matilda**; *masc* a diminutive form of **Matthew**.

Maud, Maude *fem* a medieval form of **Matilda**.

Maura *fem* an Irish form of **Mary**.

Maureen *fem* an Irish diminutive form of **Mary**.

Maurice *masc* Moorish, dark-coloured (*Latin*); a diminutive form is **Mo**.

Mauricio *masc* a Spanish form of **Maurice**.

Maurits *masc* a Dutch form of **Maurice**.

Maurizio *masc* an Italian form of **Maurice**.

Mauro *masc* the Italian form of **Maurus**.

Maurus *masc* from Mauritania, Moorish (*Latin*).

Mave *fem* a variant form of **Maeve**; a diminutive form of **Mavis**.

Mavis *fem* an alternative name of the song thrush used as a first name (*English*); a diminutive form is **Mave**.

Max *masc* a diminutive form of **Maximilian, Maxwell**, also used independently; a diminutive form is **Maxie**.

Maxie *masc* a diminutive form of **Max, Maximilian, Maxwell**; *fem* a diminutive form of **Maxine**.

Maximilian *masc* the greatest, a combination of *Maximus* and *Aemilianus* (*Latin*); diminutive forms are **Max, Maxie**.

Maximilien *masc* the French form of **Maximilian**.

Maxine *fem* form of **Max**.

Maxwell *masc* a surname, meaning spring of Magnus, used as a first name; a diminutive form is **Max**.

May *fem* diminutive form of **Margaret, Mary**; the name of the month used as a first name; a variant form is **Mae**; a diminutive form is **Minnie**.

Maybelle *fem* a compound of May and Belle; a variant form of **Mabel**.

Mayer *masc* a surname, meaning physician (*Old French*) or farmer (*Germanic*), used as a first name; variant forms are **Meyer, Myer**.

Maynard *masc* a surname, meaning strong, brave, used as a first name (*Germanic*).

Mayo *masc* a placename, meaning plain of the yew tree, used as a first name (*Irish Gaelic*).

McGee *masc* a variant form of **Magee**.

Meave *fem* a variant form of **Maeve**.

Medea *fem* meditative; in Greek mythology the princess who helped Jason obtain the Golden Fleece from her father (*Greek*).

Medwin *masc* a surname, meaning mead friend, used as a first name (*ld English*).

Meg, Meggie *fem* diminutive forms of **Margaret**.

Megan *fem Welsh* diminutive form of **Meg**, now used independently.

Mehetabel, Mehitabel *fem* benefited of God (*Hebrew*).

Meironwen *fem* white dairymaid (*Welsh*).

Mel *masc* a diminutive form of **Melville, Melvin, Melvyn**.

Melanie *fem* black (*Greek*).

Melbourne *masc* a surname, meaning mill stream, used as a first name (*Old English*).

Melchior *masc* of uncertain meaning, possibly king of light; in the Bible, one of the three kings (*Hebrew*).

Melchiorre *masc* the Italian form of **Melchior**.

Melfyn *masc* from Carmarthen (*Welsh*).

Melinda *fem* honey (*Greek*) plus the suffix -inda.

Melisande *fem* the French form of **Millicent**.

Melissa *fem* a bee (*Greek*); a diminutive form is **Lissa**.

Melody *fem* a word for tune or tunefulness used as a first name.

Melville, Melvin, Melvyn *masc* a surname, meaning Amalo's place, used as a first name (*Old French*); a diminutive form is **Mel**.

Mercedes *fem* the Spanish form of **Mercy** (as a plural),

Mercer *masc* a surname, meaning merchant, used as a first name (*Old French*).

Mercy *fem* the quality of forgiveness used as a first name (*English*).

Meredith *masc*, *fem* a surname, meaning lord, used as a first name (*Welsh*).

Merfyn *masc* eminent matter (*Welsh*).

Meri *fem* a variant form of **Merry**.

Meriel *fem* a Welsh form of **Muriel**; variant forms are **Merle, Meryl**.

Merle *masc* blackbird (*Old French*); a variant form of **Meriel**.

Merlin, Merlyn *masc* sea fort (*Welsh*).

Merri, Merrie *fem* variant forms of **Merry**.

Merrill *masc* a surname, meaning son of Muriel (*Celtic*) or pleasant place (*Old English*), used as a first name; variant forms are **Meryl, Merryll**.

Merry

Merry *fem* the adjective, meaning cheerful, mirthful, joyous, used as a first name (*Old English*); a diminutive form of **Meredith**; variant forms are **Meri, Merri, Merrie**.

Merryll *masc* a variant form of **Merrill**.

Merton *masc* a surname, meaning farmstead by the pool, used as a first name (*Old English*).

Mervin, Mervyn *masc* a surname, meaning famous friend, used as a first name (*Old English*); a variant formis **Marvin**; anglicized forms of **Merfyn**.

Meryl *fem* a variant form of **Meriel, Merrill**.

Meta *fem* a diminutive form of **Margaret**.

Meyer *masc* a variant form of **Mayer**.

Mia *fem* a diminutive form of **Maria**.

Micah *masc* who is like the Lord? (*Hebrew*).

Michael *masc* who is like God? (*Hebrew*); diminutive forms are **Mick, Micky, Mike**.

Michaela *fem* form of **Michael**.

Michaella *fem* the Italian form of **Michaela**.

Michel *masc* the French form of **Michael**; a German diminutive of **Michael**.

Michele *masc* the Italian form of **Michael**.

Michèle, Michelle *fem* French forms of **Michaela**, now used as English-language forms.

Mick, Micky *masc* diminutive forms of **Michael**.

Mignon *fem* a word, meaning sweet, dainty, used as a first name (*French*); a diminutive form is **Mignonette**; a diminutive form is **Minette**.

Miguel *masc* the Spanish and Portuguese form of **Michael**.

Mikael *masc* the Swedish form of **Michael**.

Mike *masc* a diminutive form of **Michael**.

Mikhail *masc* a Russian form of **Michael**; a diminutive form is **Mischa**.

Mil *fem* a diminutive form of **Mildred, Millicent**.

Milcah *fem* queen (*Hebrew*).

Mildred *fem* mild speaker (*Germanic*); diminutive forms are **Mil, Millie**.

Miles *masc* a soldier (*Germanic*); a variant form is **Myles**.

Milford *masc* a placename and surname, meaning mill ford, used as a first name (*Old English*).

Miller *masc* a surname, meaning miller, grinder, used as a first name (*Old English*); a variant form is **Milner**.

Millicent *fem* work and strength (*Germanic*); a diminutive form is **Millie**.

Millie *fem* diminutive form of **Amelia, Emilia, Mildred, Millicent**.

Millward *masc* a variant form of **Milward**.

Milne *masc* a surname, meaning at the mill, used as a first name (*Old English*).

Milner *masc* a variant form of **Miller**.

Milo *masc* a Latin form of **Miles**; a diminutive form of **Myles**.

Milton *masc* a surname, meaning middle farmstead or mill farm, used as a first name (*Old English*); a diminutive form is **Milt**.

Milward *masc* a surname, meaning mill keeper, used as a first name (*Old English*); a variant form is **Millward**.

Mima *fem* a diminutive form of **Jemima**.

Mimi *fem* an Italian diminutive form of **Maria**.

Mimosa *fem* the English name of a tropical shrub with yellow flowers used as a first name, from imitative (*Latin*).

Minerva *fem* wise one; in Roman mythology the counterpart of Athena, goddess of wisdom.

Minette *fem* a diminutive form of **Mignonette**..

Minna, Minne *fem* love (*Germanic*); diminutive forms of **Wilhelmina**.

Minnie *fem* a diminutive form of **Mary, May, Wilhelmina**.

Minta *fem* a diminutive form of **Araminta**.

Mira *fem* a diminutive form of **Mirabel, Miranda**.

Mirabel, Mirabelle *fem* wonderful (*Latin*); diminutive forms are **Mira, Myra**.

Miranda *fem* admirable (*Latin*); diminutive forms are **Mira, Myra**.

Miriam *fem* variant form of **Mary**.

Mischa *masc* a diminutive form of **Mikhail**.

Mitchell *masc* a surname form of **Michael**; a surname, meaning big, great, used as a first name (*Old English*).

Mitzi *fem* a German diminutive form of **Maria**.

Mo *masc fem* diminutive form of **Maureen, Maurice, Morris**.

Modest *masc* the Russian form of *modestus*, obedient (*Latin*).

Modesty *fem* an English word from *modestus* (*Latin*) for the quality of being shy or humble used as a first name.

Modred *masc* counsellor; in Arthurian legend the knight who killed King Arthur (*Old English*).

Moira *fem* an anglicized Irish form of **Mary**; a variant form is **Moyra**.

Mollie, Molly *fem* diminutive forms of **Mary**, now used independently.

Mona *fem* noble (*Irish Gaelic*).

Monica *fem* of certain meaning, but possibly advising (*Latin*).

Monika *fem* the German form of **Monica**.

Monique *fem* the French form of **Monica**, now also used as an English form.

Monroe, Monro *masc* a surname, meaning mouth of the Roe river, used as a first name (*Irish Gaelic*); variant forms are **Munro, Munroe, Munrow**.

Montague, Montagu *masc* a surname, meaning pointed hill, used as a first name; a diminutive form is **Monty**.

Montgomery, Montgomerie *masc* a surname, meaning hill of powerful man, used as a first name (*Old French/Germanic*); a diminutive form is **Monty**.

Monty *masc* a diminutive form of **Montague, Montgomery**.

Morag *fem* great (*Scots Gaelic*).

Moray *masc* a variant form of **Murray**.

Morgan *masc fem* of the sea (*Celtic*).

Morgana *fem* form of **Morgan**.

Moritz *masc* the German form of **Maurice**.

Morley *masc* a surname, meaning moor meadow, used as a first name (*Old English*).

Morna *fem* a Scots variant form of **Myrna**.

Morrice, Morris *masc* variant forms of **Maurice**; a diminutive form is **Mo**.

Mortimer *masc* a surname, meaning dead sea, used as a first name (*Old French*).

Morton *masc* a surname, meaning farmstead moor, used as a first name (*Old English*).

Morven *fem* a Scottish placename, meaning sea gap, used as a first name (*Scots Gaelic*).

Mosè *masc* the Italian form of **Moses**.

Moses *masc* drawn out of the water.

Moyra *fem a* variant form of **Moira**.

Muir *masc* a Scottish form of the surname Moore, meaning moor (*Old French*), used as a surname.

Muirne *fem* beloved (*Irish Gaelic*).

Mungo *masc* amiable (*Gaelic*).

Munro, Munroe, Munrow *masc* variant forms of **Monroe**.

Murdo, Murdoch *masc* mariner (*Scots Gaelic*).

Muriel *fem* sea bright (*Celtic*).

Murray *masc* a surname, meaning seaboard place, used as a first name; a variant form is **Moray**.

Myer *masc* a surname, meaning marsh (*Old Norse*), used a first name; a variant form of **Mayer**.

Myfanwy *fem* my fine one (*Welsh*).

Myles *masc* a variant form of **Miles**; devotee of Mary (*Irish Gaelic*).

Myra *fem* a name invented by the poet Fulke Greville, possibly as an anagram of **Mary**, or to mean she who weeps or laments (*Greek*); a diminutive form of **Mirabel, Miranda**.

Myrna *fem* beloved (*Irish Gaelic*); a variant form is **Morna**.

Myron *masc* fragrant oil (*Greek*).

Myrtle *fem* the name of the shrub used as a first name.

N

Naamah *fem* pretty, loved (*Hebrew*).

Naaman *masc* pleasant (*Hebrew*).

Nadezhda *fem* hope (*Russian*).

Nadia *fem* an English, French and Italian form of **Nadezhda**.

Nadine *fem* a French diminutive form of **Nadia**.

Nahum *masc* consoler (*Hebrew*).

Naida *fem* The water nymph (*Latin*); a diminutive form is **Naiada**.

Nairn *masc* Dweller by the alder tree (*Celtic*).

Nairne *fem* From the river (*Gaelic*).

Nan *fem* a diminutive form of **Ann, Nancy, Nanette**.

Nana *fem* a diminutive form of **Hannah**.

Nancy *fem* a diminutive form of **Ann**, now used independently; diminutive forms are **Nan, Nina**.

Nanette *fem* a diminutive form of Ann, now used independently; a diminutive form is **Nan**.

Naomi *fem* pleasantness (*Hebrew*).

Napea *fem* Girl of the valley (*Latin*); diminutive forms are **Napaea, Napia**.

Naphtali *masc* I have struggled (*Hebrew*).

Napier *masc* a surname, meaning linen keeper, used as a first name (*Old French*).

Napoleon *masc* lion of the forest dell (*Greek*); a diminutive form is **Nap**.

Nara *fem* Nearest and dearest (*English*).

Narda *fem* Fragrant perfume. The lingering essence (*Latin*).

Nash *masc* a surname, meaning ash tree, used as a first name (*Old English*).

Nat *masc* a diminutive form of **Nathan, Nathaniel**.

Natal *masc* the Spanish form of **Noël**.

Natale *masc* the Italian form of **Noël**.

Natalie *fem* a French form of **Natalya** now used as an English-language form.

Natalia *fem* a Spanish form of **Natalya**.

Natalya *fem* Christmas (*Latin/Russian*).

Natasha *fem* a Russian diminutive form of **Natalya**.

Nathan *masc* given; a gift (*Hebrew*); a diminutive form is **Nat**.

Nathania *fem* Gift of God (*Hebrew*); diminutive forms are **Natene, Nathene, Nathane**.

Nathaniel, Nathanael *masc* the gift of God (*Hebrew*); a diminutive form is **Nat**.

Neal, Neale *masc* variant forms of **Neil**.

Nebula *fem* A cloud of mist (*Latin*).

Ned, Neddie, Neddy *masc* (contraction of "mine Ed") diminutive forms of **Edgar, Edmund, Edward, Edwin**.

Nehemiah *masc* comfort of the Lord (*Hebrew*).

Neil *masc* champion (*Gaelic*); variant forms are **Neal, Neale, Nial, Niall**.

Nell, Nellie, Nelly *fem* diminutive forms of **Eleanor, Ellen, Helen**.

Nelson *masc* a surname, meaning son of Neil, used as a first name.

Nemo *masc* grove (*Greek*).

Nerice, Nerine, Nerissa *fem* from the sea (*Greek*).

Nero *masc* dark, black-haired (*Latin*).

Nerys *fem* lord (*Welsh*).

Nessa *fem* a diminutive form of **Agnes, Vanessa**.

Nessie *fem* a diminutive form of **Agnes**.

Nesta *fem* a Welsh diminutive form of **Agnes**.

Nestor *masc* coming home (*Greek*).

Netta, Nettie *fem* diminutive forms of **Henrietta**.

Neven *masc* a variant form of **Nevin**.

Neville *masc* a placename and surname, meaning new place, used as a first name (*Old French*).

Nevin *masc* a surname, meaning little saint, used as a first name (*Irish Gaelic*); variant forms are **Nevin, Niven**.

Newell *masc* a surname, meaning new field, used as a first name (*Old English*).

Newland *masc* a surname, meaning new land, used as a first name (*Old English*).

Newlyn, Newlin *masc* a placename and surname, meaning pool for a fleet, used as a first name (*Cornish*).

Newman *masc* a surname, meaning newcomer, new settler, used as a first name (*Old English*).

Newton *masc* a surname, meaning new farmstead or village, used as a first name (*Old English*).

Nial *masc* variant forms of **Neil**.

Niamh *fem* bright (*Irish Gaelic*).

Niall *masc* a variant form of **Neil**.

Nickson *masc* a variant form of **Nixon**.

Niccolò *masc* an Italian form of **Nicholas**.

Nicholas *masc* victory of the people (*Greek*); a variant form is **Nicolas**; diminutive forms are **Nick, Nicky**.

Nick *masc* a diminutive form of **Nicholas, Nicol**.

Nicky *masc* a diminutive form of **Nicholas, Nicol**; *fem* a diminutive forme of **Nicole**.

Nicodemus *masc* conqueror of the people (*Greek*).

Nicol *masc* a Scottish surname form of **Nicholas** used as a first name.

Nicola *masc* an Italian form of **Nicholas**; *fem* a variant form of **Nicole**.

Nicolas *masc* a Spanish form of **Nicholas**.

Nicole *fem* form of **Nicholas**; variant forms are **Nicola, Nicolette, Colette**; diminutive forms are **Nicky, Nikkie**.

Nigel *masc* a Latinized form of **Neil**.

Nikki *fem* a diminutive form of **Nicole**.

Nikolaus *masc* a German form of **Nicholas**.

Nils *masc* a Scandinavian form of **Neil**.

Nina *fem* a diminutive form of **Nancy**.

Ninette *fem French* a diminutive form of **Ann**.

Ninian *masc* meaning uncertain; the name of a 5th-century saint (*Celtic*).

Ninon *fem* a diminutive form of **Ann** (*French*).

Nita *fem* a diminutive form of **Anita, Juanita**.

Nixie *fem* Water sprite (*Germanic*); diminutive forms are **Nissie, Nissy**.

Nixon *masc* a surname, meaning son of Nicholas', used as a first name; a variant form is **Nickson**.

Noah *masc* rest; comfort (*Hebrew*).

Noble *masc* a surname, meaning noble, famous, used as a first name (*Old French*).

Noé *masc* the French and Spanish form of **Noah**.

Noè *masc* the Italian form of **Noah**.

Noël, Noel *masc .fem* Christmas; born on Christmas Day (*French*)

Noëlle, Noelle *fem* form of **Noël**.

Nola *fem* famous (*Irish Gaelic*).

Nolan *masc* a surname, meaning son of the champion, used as a first name (*Irish Gaelic*)..

Noll, Nollie masc diminutive forms of **Oliver**.

Nona *fem* ninth (*Latin*).

Nora, Norah *fem* a diminutive form of **Eleanor, Honora, Leonora**, also used independently.

Norbert *masc* northern hero (*Germanic*).

Noreen *fem* an Irish form of **Nora**.

Norma *fem* a rule (*Latin*), but probably invented as the name of the heroine of Bellini's opera.

Norman *masc* a northman; a native of Normandy (*Germanic*); a diminutive form is **Norrie**.

Northcliffe *masc* a surname, meaning north cliff, used as a first name (*Old English*).

Norton *masc* a surname, meaning northern farmstead or village, used as a surname (*Old English*).

Norville *masc* a surname, meaning north town, used as a first name (*Old French*).

Norvin *masc* northern friend (*Old English*).

Norward *masc* a surname, meaning northern guardian, used as a first name (*Old English*).

Norwell *masc* a surname, meaning northern stream, used as a first name.

Norwood *masc* a surname, meaning north wood, used as a first name (*Old English*).

Nowell *masc* an English form of **Noël**.

Nuala *fem* a diminutive form of **Fionnuala**, also used independently.

Nye *masc* a diminutive form of **Aneurin**.

O

Oakley *masc* a surname, meaning oak tree meadow, used as a first name (*Old English*).

Obadiah *masc* servant of the Lord (*Hebrew*).

Obed *masc* serving God (*Hebrew*).

Oberon *masc* a variant form of **Auberon**.

Obert *masc* wealthy, brilliant (*Germanic*).

Octavia *fem* form of **Octavius**.

Octavie *fem* a French form of **Octavia**.

Octavius *masc* eighth (*Latin*).

Oda *masc* a French form of **Otto**.

Odd *masc* the Norwegian form of **Otto**.

Oddo, Oddone *masc* Italian forms of **Otto**.

Oded *masc* upholder (*Hebrew*).

Odelia, Odelie *fem* variant forms of **Odile**.

Odette *fem* a diminutive form of **Oda**.

Odile, Odille *fem* rich, wealthy (*Germanic*); variant forms are **Odelia, Odelie, Ottilie, Otilie**.

Odoardo *masc* an Italian form of **Edward**.

Ofra *fem* a variant form of **Ophrah**.

Ogden *masc* a surname, meaning oak valley, used as first name (*Old English*).

Ogilvie, Ogilvy *masc* a surname, meaning high peak, used as a first name (*Celtic*).

Olaf, Olav *masc* ancestor heirs (*Old Norse*).

Oleg *masc* the Russian form of **Helge**.

Olga *fem* the Russian form of **Helga**.

Olimpia *fem* the Italian form of **Olympia**.

Olive *fem* an olive (*Latin*); a variant form is **Olivia**.

Oliver *masc* an olive tree (*Latin*); diminutive forms are **Ollie, Olly, Noll, Nollie**.

Oliverio *masc* the spanish form of **Oliver**.

Olivia *fem* a variant form of **Olive**; a diminutive form is **Livia**.

Oliviero *masc* the Italian form of **Oliver**.

Ollie, Olly *masc* diminutive forms of **Oliver**.

Olwen *fem* white track (*Welsh*).

Olympe *fem* the French form of **Olympia**.

Olympia *fem* heavenly (*Greek*).

Omar *masc* first son (*Arabic*).

Ona *fem* a diminutive form of names ending -ona, e.g. Fiona.

Onefre *masc* a Spanish form of **Humphrey**.

Onefredo *masc* an Italian form of **Humphrey**.

Onfroi *masc* a French form of **Humphrey**.

Onofrio *masc* the Italian form of **Humphrey**.

Onorio *masc* the Italian form of **Honorius**.

Oona, Oonagh *fem* variant forms of **Una**.

Opal *fem* the name of the iridescent gemstone used as a first name, precious stone (*Sanskrit*).

Ophelia

Ophelia *fem* a help; useful (*Greek*).

Ophélie *fem* the French form of **Ophelia**.

Ophrah, Ophra *fem* fawn (*Hebrew*); variant forms are
    Ofra, Oprah.

Oprah *fem* a modern variant of **Ophrah**.

Oran *masc* pale-skinned man (*Irish Gaelic*); variant
    forms are **Orin, Orrin**.

Orazio *masc* the Italian form of **Horace**.

Oren *masc* laurel (*Hebrew*).

Oreste *masc* the Italian form of **Orestes**.

Orestes *masc* mountain climber; in Greek mythology the
    son of Agnamemnon, who killed his mother and her
    lover in revenge for the death of his father. (*Greek*).

Orfeo *masc* the Italian form of **Orpheus**.

Oriana, Oriane *fem* golden (*Latin*).

Oriel *fem* strife (*Germanic*).

Orin *masc* a variant form of **Oran**.

Orion *masc* son of light (*Greek*).

Orla *fem* golden girl (*Irish Gaelic*).

Orlanda *fem* form of **Orlando**.

Orlando *masc* the Italian form of **Roland**.

Ormond, Ormonde *masc* a surname, meaning from east
    Munster, used as a first name (*Irish Gaelic*).

Orna *fem* form or **Oran**.

Orpheus *masc* of undertain meaning; in Greek mythol-
    ogy, a poet who sought to retrieve his wife Eurydice
    from Hades.

Orrin *masc* a variant form of **Oran**.

Orso *masc* bear (*Latin/Italian*).

Orsola *fem* the Italian form of **Ursula**.

Orson *masc* little bear (*Latin/Old French*).

Ortensia *fem* the Italian form of **Hortense**.

Orville, Orvil *masc* golden place (*Old French*).

Orwin *masc* a variant form of **Erwin**.

Osbert *masc* god-bright (*Old English*); a diminutive form
is **Ossie**.

Osborn, Osborne, Osbourne *masc* a surname, meaning divine warrior (*Old English*) or divine bear (*Old
Norse*), used as a surname; a diminutive form is **Ossie**.

Oscar *masc* leaping warrior (*Celtic*); a diminutive form
is **Ossie**.

Oskar *masc* the German and Scandinavian form of **Oscar**.

Osmond, Osmund *masc* protection of God (*Germanic*); a diminutive form is **Ossie**.

Ossie *masc* a diminutive form of **Osbert, Osborn, Oscar, Osmond, Oswald**.

Osvaldo *masc* the Italian form of **Oswald**.

Oswald *masc* power of God (*Germanic*).

Oswin *masc* god-friend (*Old English*).

Otis *masc* a surname, meaning son of Ote, used as a first
name (*Germanic*).

Ottavia *fem* the Italian form of **Octavia**.

Ottavio *masc* the Italian form of **Octavius**.

Ottilie, Otilie *fem* variant forms of **Odile**.

Otto *masc* rich (*Germanic*).

Ottone

Ottone *masc* an Italian form of **Otto**.

Owain *masc* a Welsh form of **Eugene**.

Owen *masc* a lamb; a young warrior (*Celtic*).

Oxford *masc* a placename, meaning ford for oxen, used as a first name (*Old English*).

Oxton *masc* a surname, meaning place for keeping oxen, used as a first name (*Old English*).

Oz, Ozzie, Ozzy *masc* diminutive forms of names beginning with *Os-*.

P

Pablo *masc* the Spanish form of **Paul**.

Paddy *masc* a diminutive form of **Patrick**; fem a diminutive form of **Patricia**.

Padraig *masc* the Irish Gaelic form of **Patrick**.

Paget, Pagett, Padget, Padgett *masc* a surname, meaning young page, used as a first name (*Old French*).

Paige, Page *fem* a surname, meaning page, used as a first name (*Old French*).

Palmiro *masc* palm (*Latin*).

Palmira *fem* form of **Palmiro**.

Paloma *fem* the Spanish word for dove used as a first name.

Pamela *fem* a name invented by the poet Sir Philip Sidney derived from the Greek work for honey; a diminutive form is **Pam**.

Pancho *masc* a diminutive form of **Francisco**.

Pandora *fem* gifted (*Greek*); in Greek mythology, the first woman on earth.

Pansy *fem* thought (*French*); the name of the garden flower used as a first name.

Paola *fem* the Italian form of **Paula**.

Paolo *masc* the Italian form of **Paul**.

Pascal *masc* born at Easter (*Latin/French*).

Pasquale *masc* the Italian form of **Pascal**.

Pat *masc* a diminutive form of **Patrick**; fem a diminutive form of **Patricia**.

Patience *fem* patience (*Latin*).

Patric *masc* a variant form of **Patrick**.

Patrice *masc* the French form of **Patrick**; *fem* the French form of **Patricia**.

Patricia *fem* form of **Patrick**; diminutive forms are **Paddy, Pat, Patsy, Pattie, Patty, Tricia**.

Patricio *masc* the Spanish form of **Patrick**.

Patricius *masc* a variant form of **Patrick**.

Patrick *masc* noble; a patrician (*Latin*); variant forms are **Patric, Patricius**; diminutive forms are **Paddy, Pat**.

Patrizia *fem* the Italian form of **Patricia**.

Patrizio *masc* the Italian form of **Patrick**.

Patrizius *masc* the German form of **Patrick**.

Patsy *fem* a diminutive form of **Patricia**.

Pattie, Patty *fem* diminutive forms of **Martha, Patience, Patricia**.

Paul *masc* little (*Latin*).

Paula *fem* form of **Paul**.

Paulette *fem* a French form of **Paula**.

Paulina, Pauline *fem* diminutive forms of **Paula**.

Payne *masc* a surname, meaning countryman, used as a first name.

Peace *fem* the word for the condition of tranquillity or calm used as a first name (*Latin*).

Pearl *fem* the name of the lustrous white gem used as a first name.

Pedaiah *masc* Jehovah ransoms (*Hebrew*).

Pedro *masc* the Portuguese and Spanish form of **Peter**.

Peer *masc* a Norwegian form of **Peter**.

Peg, Peggie, Peggy *fem* diminutive forms of **Margaret**.

Peleg *masc* division (*Hebrew*).

Penelope *fem* duck (*Greek*); diminutive forms are **Pen, Penny**.

Penny *fem* diminutive form of **Penelope**, now used independently.

Peony *fem* healing (*Greek*), the name of a plant with pink, red, white or yellow flowers used as a first name.

Pepe *masc* a diminutive form of **José**.

Pepin *masc* enduring (*Germanic*).

Pepillo, Pepito *masc* diminutive forms of **José**.

Per *masc* a Scandinavian form of **Peter**.

Percival, Perceval *masc* pierce valley (*Old French*).

Percy *masc* a surname, meaning from Perci-en-Auge in Normandy, used as a first name (*Old French*).

Perdita *fem* lost (*Latin*), invented by Shakespeare for a character in *The Winter's Tale*.

Peregrine *masc* stranger, pilgrim (*Latin*); a diminutive form is **Perry**.

Peronel *fem* a contraction of **Petronel**.

Perry *masc* diminutive form of **Peregrine**, now used in its own right; a surname, meaning pear tree, used as a first name (*Old English*).

Persephone *fem* of uncertain meaning; in Greek mythology, goddess of the underworld (*Greek*).

Persis *fem* a Persian woman (*Greek*).

Peter *masc* a rock (*Latin*); diminutive forms are **Pete**, **Peterkin**.

Petra *fem* form of **Peter**.

Petrina *fem* a diminutive form of **Petra**.

Petronel, Petronella *fem* form of Petronius, a Roman family name (*Latin*).

Petrus *masc* a German form of Peter.

Petula *fem* asking (*Latin*); a diminutive form is **Pet**.

Petunia *fem* the name of a plant with white, blue or purple flowers used as a first name.

Phebe *fem* a variant form of **Phoebe**.

Phedra *fem* bright (*Greek*).

Phèdre *fem* the French form of **Phedra**.

Phelim *masc* always good (*Irish*).

Phemie, Phamie *fem* diminutive forms of **Euphemia**.

Phenie *fem* a diminutive form of **Josephine**.

Phil *masc* a diminutive form of **Philip, Phillip**; *fem* a diminutive form of **Philippa**.

Philbert *masc* very bright (*Germanic*).

Philemon *masc* loving; friendly (*Greek*).

Philip *masc* lover of horses (*Greek*); a variant form is **Phillip**; diminutive forms are **Phil, Pip**.

Philipp *masc* the German form of **Philip**.

Philippa *fem* form of **Philip**; diminutive forms are **Phil, Pippa**.

Philippe *masc* the French form of **Philip**.

Phillip *masc* a a variant form of **Philip**; diminutive forms are **Phil, Pip**.

Philomena *fem* love and strength (*Greek*).

Phineas, Phinehas *masc* mouth of brass (*Hebrew*).

Phoebe *fem* pure; radiant (*Greek*); a variant form is **Phebe**.

Phyllida *fem* a variant form of **Phyllis**.

Phyllis *fem* a green bough (*Greek*).

Pia *fem* form of **Pio**.

Pierce *masc* a surname form of Piers used as a first name.

Pierre *masc* the French form of **Peter**.

Piers *masc* a variant form of **Peter**.

Pierse *masc* a surname form of Piers used as a first name.

Pieter *masc* a Dutch form of **Peter**.

Pietro *masc* the Italian form of **Peter**.

Pilar *fem* pillar (*Spanish*), an allusion to the Virgin Mary who appeared to St James the Greater standing on a pillar.

Pio *masc* the Italian form of **Pius**.

Pip *masc.* a diminutive form of **Philip, Phillip**; *fem* a diminutive form of **Philippa**.

Pippa *fem* a diminutive form of **Philippa**.

Pius *masc* holy (*Latin*).

Placido *masc* peaceful (*Latin/Spanish*).

Plato *masc* broad (*Greek*).

Polly *fem* diminutive form of **Mary**, now used independently.

Pollyanna *fem* a compound of **Polly** and **Anna**.

Pomona *fem* fruitful (*Latin*).

Poppy *fem* the name of the plant that has bright red flower used as a first name.

Portia *fem* gift (*Latin*).

Presley *masc* a surname, meaning priests' meadow, used as a first name.

Prima *fem* form of **Primo**.

Primo *masc* first born (*Latin*).

Primrose *fem* the name of the yellow spring flower used as a first name.

Priscilla *fem* somewhat old; ancient (*Latin*); diminutive forms are **Cilla, Prissie**.

Prosper *masc* favourable, fortunate (*Latin*).

Pròspero *masc* the Italian form of **Prosper**.

Prudence *fem* the word for the quality of caution or circumspection used as a first name (*Latin*); diminutive forms are **Prue, Prudie**.

Prue *fem* a diminutive form of **Prudence, Prunella**.

Prunella *fem* plum (*Latin*); a diminutive form is **Prue**.

Psyche *fem* of the soul (*Greek*).

Pugh *masc* a surname, meaning son of Hugh, used as a first name (*Welsh*).

Q

Queenie *fem* a diminutive form of the word queen, the supreme woman, used as a first name (*Old English*).

Quenby *fem* a surname, meaning queen's manor, used as a first name (*Old English*).

Quentin *masc* fifth (*Latin*); a variant form is **Quinton**.

Querida *fem* beloved, a Spanish term of endearment used as a first name.

Quinta *fem* form of **Quinto**.

Quinto *masc* the Italian form of **Quintus**.

Quintus *masc* fifth-born (*Latin*).

Quenel, Quennel *masc* a surname, meaning queen war, used as a first name (*Old English*).

Quigley, Quigly *masc* a surname, meaning untidy, used as a first name (*Irish Gaelic*).

Quinby *masc* a variant form of **Quenby**.

Quincy, Quincey *masc* a surname, meaning fifth place, used as a first name (*Latin/French*).

Quinlan *masc* well formed (*Irish Gaelic*).

Quinn *masc* a surname, meaning wise, used as a first name (*Irish Gaelic*).

Quinton *masc* a variant form of **Quentin**.

R

Rab, Rabbie *masc* diminutive forms of **Robert**.

Raban *masc* raven (*Germanic*).

Rachel *fem* a ewe; a lamb (*Hebrew*); a variant form is **Rachelle**; diminutive forms are **Rae, Ray**.

Rachele *fem* the Italian form of **Rachel**.

Rachelle *fem* a variant form of **Rachel**.

Radcliffe *masc* a surname, meaning red cliff, used as a first name (*Old English*).

Radley *masc* a surname, meaning red meadow, used as a first name (*Old English*).

Radnor *masc* a placename and surname, meaning red slopes, used as a first name (*Old English*).

Rae *fem* a diminutive form of **Rachel**.

Rafe *masc* a variant form of **Ralph**.

Raffaele, Raffaello *masc* Italian forms of **Raphael**.

Rafferty *masc* a surname, meaning prosperous, used as a first name (*Irish Gaelic*).

Rahel *fem* a German form of **Rachel**.

Raimondo *masc* the Italian form of **Raymond**.

Raimund *masc* the German form of **Raymond**.

Raimundo *masc* a Spanish form of **Raymond**.

Rainaldo *masc* an Italian form of **Reginald**.

Rainier *masc* a French form of **Rayner**.

Raisa *fem* tolerant (*Greek*).

Raleigh *masc* a surname, meaning red or deer meadow, used as a first name (*Old English*); variant forms are **Rawley, Rayleigh**.

Ralph *masc* famous wolf or hero (*Germanic*); variant forms are **Rafe, Rolph**.

Ram *masc* height (*Hebrew*).

Ramón *masc* a Spanish form of **Raymond**.

Ramona *fem* form of **Ramón**.

Ramsden *masc* Ram's valley (*Old English*).

Ramsay, Ramsey *masc* a placename and surname, meaning wild garlic river island, used as a first name (*Old Norse*).

Ranald *masc* a variant form of **Reginald**.

Rand *masc* a diminutive form of **Randal, Randolf**.

Randal, Randall *masc* a surname diminutive form of **Randolph** used as a first name (*Old English*); a variant form is **Ranulf**.

Randolf, Randolph *masc* shield-wolf (*Germanic*); a variant form is **Ranulf**; diminutive forms are **Rand, Randy**.

Randy *masc* a diminutive form of **Randolf**, also used independently.

Ranee, Rani *fem* queen (*Hindi*).

Rankin, Rankine *masc* a diminutive surname form of **Randolph** used as a first name.

Ransom *masc* a surname, meaning son of Rand, used as a first name.

Ranulf *masc* a variant form of **Randolf**.

Raoul *masc* the French form of **Ralph**.

Raphael *masc* the healing of God (*Hebrew*).

Raphaela *fem* form of **Raphael**.

Raquel *fem* the Spanish form of **Rachel**.

Ras *masc* a diminutive form of **Erasmus, Erastus**.

Rasmus *masc* a diminutive form of **Erasmus**.

Rastus *masc* a diminutive form of **Erastus**.

Rawley *masc* a variant form of **Raleigh**.

Rawnsley *masc* a surname, meaning Raven's meadow, used as a first name (*Old English*).

Ray *masc* a diminutive form of **Raymond**, now used independently; *fem* a diminutive form of **Rachel**; a variant form is **Rae**.

Rayleigh *masc* a variant form of **Raleigh**.

Raymond, Raymund *masc* wise protection (*Germanic*); a diminutive form is **Ray**.

Rayne *masc, fem* a surname, meaning mighty army, used as a first name; variant forms are **Raine** (*fem*), **Rayner** (*masc*).

Rayner *masc* a variant form of **Rayne** (*Germanic*).

Rea *fem* a variant form of **Rhea**.

Read, Reade *masc* a surname, meaning red headed, used as a first name(*Old English*); variant forms are **Reed, Reede**.

Reading *masc* a placename and surname, meaning peo-

ple of the red one, used as a first name; a variant form
is **Redding**.

Reagan *masc* a variant form of **Regan**.

Reardon *masc* a variant form of **Riordan**.

Rebecca, Rebekah *fem* a cow, denoting domestic ability or value (*Hebrew*); diminutive forms are **Beckie,
Becky**.

Redding *masc* a variant form of **Reading**.

Redman *masc* a surname, meaning red cairn or thatch-
er, used as a first name (*Old English*); a variant form
of **Redmond**.

Redmond *masc* an Irish form of **Raymond**; a variant
form is **Redman**.

Reece *masc* a surname form of **Rhys** used as a first name.

Reed, Reede *masc* variant forms of **Read**.

Rees *masc* the English form of **Rhys**.

Reeve, Reeves *masc* steward, bailiff (*Old English*).

Regan *masc*, *fem* a surname, meaning little king, used
as a first name (*Irish Gaelic*); variant forms are **Reagan, Rogan**.

Regina *fem* queen (*Latin*).

Reginald *masc* strong ruler (*Germanic*); diminutive
forms are **Reg, Reggie**.

Reilly *masc* a surname, meaning valiant, used as a first
name (*Irish Gaelic*); a variant form is **Riley**

Reinald *masc* an early English form of **Reginald**.

Reine *fem* queen (*French*).

Reinhard *masc* a German form of **Reynard**.

Reinhold *masc* a Scandinavian form of **Reginald**.

Reinold *masc* a Dutch form of **Reginald**.

Remus *masc* power (*Latin*).

Renaldo *masc* a Spanish form of **Reginald**.

Renata *fem* a diminutive form of **Renée**.

Renato *masc* an Italian and Spanish form of **Reginald**.

Renatus *masc* the Latin form of **René**.

Renault *masc* a French form of **Reginald**.

René *masc* born again (*French*).

Renée *fem* form of **René**.

Renfrew *masc* a placename and surname, meaning point of the torrent, used as a first name (*Celtic*).

Rennie, Renny *masc* a diminutive surname form of Reynold used as a first name.

Renton *masc* a surname, meaning farmstead of Power, used as a first name (*Old English*).

Reuben *masc* behold, a son (*Hebrew*); a diminutive form is **Rube**.

Reuel *masc* friend of God.

Reva *fem* form of **Reeve**.

Rex *masc* king (*Latin*).

Rexanne *fem* a compound of **Rex** and **Anne**; a variant form of **Roxanne**.

Reynard *masc* brave advice (*Germanic*); fox (*French*).

Reynold *masc* strong rule (*Germanic*).

Rhea, Rheia *fem* of uncertain origin and meaning; in Roman mythology she was the mother of Remus and Romulus; in Greek mythology she was the mother of several gods, including Zeus; a variant form is **Rea**.

Rhiain *fem* maiden (*Welsh*).

Rhiannon *fem* goddess (*Welsh*).

Rhoda *fem* a rose (*Greek*).

Rhodri *masc* circle ruler (*Welsh*).

Rhona *fem* a variant form of **Rona**.

Rhys *masc* ardour (*Welsh*).

Ria *fem* a German diminutive form of **Maria**.

Rica *fem* a diminutive form of **Roderica**.

Ricardo *masc* a Spanish form of **Richard**.

Riccardo *masc* an Italian form of **Richard**.

Rich masc a diminutive form of **Richard, Richmond**.

Richard *masc* a strong king; powerful (*Germanic*); diminutive forms are **Dick, Rich, Richey, Richie, Rick, Rickie, Ricky, Ritchie**.

Richey, Richie *masc* diminutive forms of **Richard, Richmond**.

Richmond *masc* a surname, meaning strong hill, used as a first name (*Old French*); diminutive forms are **Rich, Richey, Richie**.

Rider *masc* a surname, meaning knight, rider, used as a first name (*Old English*).

Ridley *masc* a surname, meaning cleared meadow, used as a first name (*Old English*).

Rigby *masc* a surname, meaning farm on a ridge, used as first name (*Old English*).

Rigg *masc* a surname, meaning at the ridge, used as a first name (*Old English*).

Riley *masc* a variant form of **Reilly**.

Rina *fem* a diminutive form of names ending -rina.

Rinaldo *masc* an Italian form of **Reginald**.

Ring *masc* a surname, meaning wearing a ring, used as a first name (*Old English*).

Riordan *masc* a surname, meaning bard, used as a first name (*Irish Gaelic*); a variant form is **Reardon**.

Ripley *masc* a placename and surname, meaning strip-shaped clearing, used as a first name (*Old English*).

Rita *fem* a diminutive form of **Margarita, Margherita**, used independently.

Ritchie *masc* a diminutive and surname form of **Richard**.

Ritter *masc* knight or rider (*Germanic*).

Roald *masc* famous ruler (*Old Norse*).

Robert *masc* bright in fame (*Germanic*); diminutive forms are **Bob, Bobby, Rab, Rob, Robbie, Robby, Robin**.

Roberta *fem* form of **Robert**.

Roberto *masc* the Italian and Spanish form of **Robert**.

Robin *masc, fem* a diminutive form of **Robert**, now used independently; a variant form is **Robyn**.

Robina *fem* form of **Robin**.

Robinson *masc* a surname, meaning son of Robert, used as a first name (*Old English*).

Robyn *masc, fem* a variant form of **Robin**.

Rocco *masc* of uncertain meaning, possibly crow (*Germanic*).

Rochelle *fem* little rock (*French*).

Rochester *masc* a placename, and surname, meaning Roman fort at the bridges, used as a surname (*Old English*).

Rock *masc* stone or oak (*Old English*).

Rocky *masc* an English form of **Rocco**.

Rod *masc* a diminutive form of **Roderick, Rodney**.

Rodden *masc* a surname, meaning valley of deer, used as a first name (*Old English*).

Roddy *masc* a diminutive form of **Roderick, Rodney**.

Roderica *fem* form of Roderick; a variant form is **Rodericka**; a diminutive form is **Rica**.

Roderich *masc* the German form of **Roderick**.

Roderick, Roderic *masc* rich in fame (*Germanic*); diminutive forms are **Rod, Roddy, Rurik**.

Roderico *masc* an Italian form of **Roderick**.

Rodger *masc* a variant form of **Roger**.

Rodney *masc fem* a surname and placename, of unknown meaning, used as a first name; a diminutive form is **Rod**.

Rodolf *masc* an Italian and Spanish form of **Rudolph**.

Rodolphe *masc* a French form of **Rudolph**.

Rodrigo *masc* an Italian and Spanish form of **Roderick**.

Rodrigue *masc* the French form of **Roderick**.

Rogan *masc* a variant form of **Regan**.

Roger *masc* famous with the spear (*Germanic*); a variant form is **Rodger**.

Rogerio *masc* the Spanish form of **Roger**.

Rohan

Rohan *masc* healing, incense (*Sanskrit*).

Rohanna *fem* form of **Rohan**.

Róisín, Roisin *fem* an Irish form of **Rose**.

Roland *masc* fame of the land (*Germanic*); variant forms are **Rolland, Rowland**; a diminutive form is **Roly**.

Rolanda, Rolande *fem* forms of **Roland**.

Roldán, Rolando *masc* Spanish forms of **Roland**.

Rolf *masc* a contraction of **Rudolf**; a variant form is **Rollo**.

Rolland *masc* a variant form of **Roland**.

Rollo *masc* a variant form of **Rolf**.

Rolph *masc* a variant form of **Ralph**.

Roly *masc* a diminutive form of **Roland**.

Roma *fem* a Roman (*Latin*).

Romeo *masc* a Roman (*Latin*).

Romilly *masc* a surname, meaning broad clearing (*Old English*) or place of Romilius (*Old French*), used as a first name

Romney *masc* a placename, meaning at the broad river, used as a first name (*Old English*).

Ròmolo *masc* the Italian form of Romulus, of Etruscan origin and unknown meaning; in Roman legend, Romulus and his brother Remus founded Rome.

Romy *fem* a diminutive form of **Rosemary**.

Ron *masc* a diminutive form of **Ronald**.

Rona *fem* the name of a Scottish island, meaning rough rocky island, used as a first name (*Old Norse*); a variant form is **Rhona**.

Ronald *masc* a variant form of **Reginald**; diminutive forms are **Ron, Ronnie, Ronny**.

Ronalda *fem* form of **Ronald**; diminutive forms are **Ronnie, Ronny**.

Ronan *masc* little seal (*Irish Gaelic*).

Ronnie, Ronny *masc* diminutive forms of **Ronald**; *fem* diminutive forms of **Ronalda, Veronica**.

Rooney *masc* red, red-complexioned (*Gaelic*).

Rory *masc* red (*Irish and Scots Gaelic*).

Rosa *fem* a rose (*Latin*); diminutive forms are **Rosetta, Rosie**.

Rosabel, Rosabella, Rosabelle *fem* a compound of **Rosa** and **Bella**.

Rosalie, Rosalia *fem* little and blooming rose.

Rosalind, Rosaline *fem* beautiful as a rose (*Latin*); a diminutive form is **Linda**.

Rosamund, Rosamond *fem* horse protection; famous protection (*Germanic*); rose of the world (*Latin*).

Rosanne, Rosanna *fem* compounds of **Rose** and **Anne**; variant forms are **Roseanne, Roseanna**.

Roscoe *masc* a surname, meaning deer wood, used as a first name (*Old Norse*).

Rose *fem* the English form of **Rosa**; the name of the flower used as a first name; diminutive forms are **Rosette, Rosie**.

Roseanne, Roseanna *fem* variant forms of **Rosanne, Rosanna**.

Rosemarie *fem* a combination of **Rose** and **Marie**.

Rosemary *fem* the name of the plant associated with re-
membrance used as a first name; diminutive forms are
Romy, Rosie.

Rosemonde *fem* a French form of **Rosamund**.

Rosetta *fem* a diminutive form of **Rosa**.

Rosette *fem* a diminutive form of **Rose**.

Rosh *masc* head (*Hebrew*).

Rosie *fem* a diminutive form of **Rosa, Rose, Rosemary**,
now also used independently.

Roslin, Roslyn *masc, fem* a placename, meaning un-
ploughable land by the pool, used as first name (*Scots
Gaelic*); a variant form is **Rosslyn**.

Rosmunda *fem* the Italian form of **Rosamund**.

Ross *masc* a placename and surname, meaning promon-
tory or moorland, used as a first name (*Scots Gaelic*).

Rosslyn *masc, fem* a variant form of **Roslin**.

Rowan *masc* red (*Irish Gaelic*).

Rowe *masc* a surname, meaning hedgerow, used as a first
name (*Old English*).

Rowell *masc* a surname, meaning rough hill, used as a
first name (*Old English*).

Rowena *fem* fame and joy (*Germanic*).

Rowland *masc* a variant form of **Roland**.

Rowley *masc* a surname, meaning rough meadow, used
as a first name (*Old English*).

Roxanne, Roxane *fem* dawn of day (*Persian*); a variant
form is **Rexanne**; a diminutive form is **Roxie**.

Roxburgh *masc* a placename and surname, meaning

Rook's fortress, used as a first name (*Old English*).

Roy *masc* red (*Gaelic*); king (*Old French*).

Royal *masc* a variant form of **Royle**; *fem* the adjective meaning befitting a monarch, regal, used as a first name.

Royce *masc* a surname form of **Rose** used as a first name.

Royle *masc* a surname, meaning rye hill, used as a first name (*Old English*); a variant form is **Royal**.

Royston *masc* a surname, meaning place of Royce, used as a first name (*Germanic/Old English*).

Rube *masc* a diminutive form of **Reuben**.

Rubén *masc* a Spanish form of **Reuben**.

Ruby *fem* the name of the red gemstone used as a first name.

Rudi *masc* German a diminutive form of **Rüdiger, Rudolf**.

Rüdiger *masc* the German form of **Roger**.

Rudolf, Rudolph *masc* famous wolf; hero (*Germanic*).

Rudyard *masc* reed enclosure (*Old English*).

Rufe *masc* a diminutive form of Rufus.

Rufus *masc* red; red-haired (*Latin*); a diminutive form is **Rufe**.

Rugby *masc* a placename and surname, meaning Hroca's stronghold, used as a first name (*Old English*).

Ruggiero, Ruggero *masc* Italian forms of **Roger**.

Rupert *masc* an anglicized Germanic form of **Robert**.

Ruprecht *masc* the German form of **Robert**.

Rurik *masc* a diminutive form of **Roderick, Roderic**.

Russell

Russell *masc* a surname meaning, red face or hair, used as a first name (*Old French*); a diminutive form is **Russ**.

Rutger *masc* a Dutch form of **Roger**.

Ruth *fem* of uncertain meaning, possibly beauty (*Hebrew*).

Rutherford *masc* a surname, meaning cattle ford, used as a first name (*Old English*).

Rutland *masc* a placename, meaning Rota's estate, used as a first name (*Old English*).

Ruy *masc* a Spanish form of **Roderick**.

Ryan *masc* the Irish surname of uncertain meaning used as a first name.

Rye *masc* From the riverbank (*French*).

Rylan, Ryland *masc* a surname, meaning where rye grows, used as a first name (*Old English*).

S

Sabin *masc* a shortened form of **Sabinus**.

Sabina *fem* Sabine woman (*Latin*).

Sabine *fem* a French and German form of **Sabina**.

Sabino *masc* an Italian form of **Sabinus**.

Sabinus *masc* Sabine man (*Latin*); a shortened form is **Sabin**.

Sabra *fem* restful (*Hebrew*).

Sabrina *fem* of uncertain meaning, linked to the name of the River Severn (*pre-Celtic*); a variant form is **Zabrina**.

Sadie *fem* a diminutive form of **Sara**.

Sal *fem* a diminutive form of **Sally, Sarah**.

Salina *fem* From the salty place (*Greek*).

Sally, Sallie *fem* diminutive forms of **Sara**, now used independently.

Salome *fem* peaceful (*Hebrew*).

Salomon *masc* the French form of **Solomon**.

Salomo *masc* a Dutch and German form of **Solomon**.

Salomone *masc* the Italian form of **Solomon**.

Salvador *masc* Christ the saviour (*Latin/Spanish*).

Salvatore *masc* the Italian form of **Salvador**.

Salvia *fem* sage (*Latin*).

Sam *masc* a diminutive form of **Samuel**, now used independently; *fem* a diminutive form of **Samantha**.

Samantha *fem* meaning obscure, possibly listener (*Aramic*) or a compound of **Sam** and **Anthea**; a diminutive form is **Sam**.

Sammy *masc* a diminutive form of **Samuel**.

Samson, Sampson *masc* splendid sun; great joy and felicity (*Hebrew*).

Samuel *masc* heard by God (*Hebrew*); diminutive forms are **Sam, Sammy**.

Samuele *masc* the Italian form of **Samuel**.

Samuela *fem* form of **Samuel**.

Sancha, Sanchia *fem* variant forms of **Sancia**.

Sancho *masc* holy (*Spanish*).

Sancia *fem* form of **Sancho**; variant form are **Sancha, Sanchia**.

Sanders *masc* son of Alexander (*Old English*); a diminutive form is **Sandy**.

Sandie *fem* a diminutive form of **Alexandra**.

Sandra *fem* a diminutive form of **Alessandra, Alexandra**, now used independently.

Sandy *masc* a diminutive form of **Alexander, Lysander, Sanders**; *fem* a diminutive form of **Alexandra**.

Sanford *masc* a surname, meaning sandy ford, used as a first name (*Old English*).

Sanson *masc* the German form of **Samson**.

Sansón *masc* the Spanish form of **Samson**.

Sansone *masc* the Italian form of **Samson**.

Santo *masc* saint (*Italian*).

Sapphire *fem* beloved of Saturn (*Sanskrit*), the name of the blue precious stone used as a first name.

Sarah, Sara *fem* a princess (*Hebrew*); diminutive forms are **Sadie, Sal, Sally**.

Saul *masc* asked for by God (*Hebrew*).

Savanna *fem* a form of the word for an open grassland used as a first name (*Spanish*).

Saveur *masc* the French form of **Salvador**.

Saxon *masc* people of the short swords (*Germanic*).

Scarlett *fem* a variation of the word scarlet (fine cloth *Old French*), a bright red colour, used as a first name by Margaret Mitchell in her novel *Gone with the Wind*.

Scott *masc* a surname, meaning of Scotland, used as a first name.

Sealey *masc* a variant form of **Seeley**.

Seamas, Seamus *masc* Irish Gaelic forms of **James**.

Sean *masc* an Irish Gaelic form of **John**.

Searle *masc* a surname, meaning armed warrior, used as a surname (*Germanic*).

Seaton *masc* a placename and surname, meaning farmstead at the sea, used as a first name (*Old English*); a variant form is **Seton**.

Sebastian *masc* man of Sebasta in Asia Minor (*Greek*).

Sebastiano *masc* the Italian form of **Sebastian**.

Sébastien *masc* the French form of **Sebastian**.

Secondo *masc* the Italian form of **Secundus**.

Secundus *masc* second born (*Latin*).

Seeley *masc* a first name, meaning blessed and happy, used as a first name (*Old English*); a variant form is **Sealey**.

Seigneur *masc* a variant form of **Senior**.

Selby *masc* a placename and surname, meaning place by the willow trees, used as a first name (*Old English*).

Selden *masc* From the valley of the willow tree (*Old English*).

Selig *masc* blessed, happy one (*Yiddish*); a variant form is **Zelig**.

Selina, Selena *fem* parsley; heavenly (*Greek*); a diminutive form is **Lina**.

Selma *fem* form of **Anselm**.

Selwyn, Selwin *masc* wild (Old French) (*Germanic*).

Semele *fem* single (*Latin*).

Senga *fem* slender (*Gaelic*); backward spelling of **Agnes**.

Senior *masc* a surname, meaning lord, used as a first name (*Old French*); a variant form is **Seigneur**.

Seonaid *fem* a Gaelic form of **Janet**.

Septima *fem* form of **Septimus**.

Septimus *masc* seventh (*Latin*).

Seraphina, Serafina *fem* of the seraphim, of burning faith (*Hebrew*).

Serena *fem* calm; peaceful (*Latin*).

Serge *masc* the French form of **Sergius**.

Sergei *masc* the Russian form of **Sergius**.

Sergio *masc* the Italian form of **Sergius**.

Sergius *masc* a Roman family name of Etruscan origin and unknown meaning.

Sesto *masc* the Italian form of **Sextus**.

Seth *masc* appointed (*Hebrew*).

Seton *masc* a variant form of **Seaton**..

Seumas *masc* a Gaelic form of **James**.

Sewald, Sewall, Sewell, *masc* a surname, meaning sea powerful, used as a first name (*Old English*); a variant form is **Siwald**.

Sexton *masc* a surname, meaning sacristan, used as a first name (*Old French*).

Sextus *masc* sixth (*Latin*).

Seymour *masc* a surname, meaning from Saint-Maur in France, used as a first name (*Old French*).

Shalom *masc* peace (*Hebrew*).

Shamus *masc* an anglicized form of **Seamus**.

Shane *masc* an anglicized form of **Sean**.

Shanley *masc* a surname, meaning son of the hero, used as a first name (*Irish Gaelic*).

Shannon *fem* the name of the Irish river, meaning the old one, used as a first name.

Shari *fem* a diminutive form of **Sharon**.

Sharon *fem* a Biblical placename mentioned in the Song of Solomon used as a first name (*Hebrew*); a diminutive form is **Shari**.

Shaw *masc* a surname, meaning small wood or grove, used as a first name (*Old English*).

Shawn, Shaun *masc* anglicized forms of **Sean**.

Shea *masc* a surname, meaning stately, dauntless, used as a first name (*Irish Gaelic*).

Sheelagh *fem* a variant form of **Sheila**.

Sheelah *fem* petition (*Hebrew*); a variant form of **Sheila**.

Sheena *fem* an anglicized form of **Sine**.

Sheffield *masc* a placename, meaning open land by the Sheaf river, used as a first name (*Old English*).

Sheila, Shelagh *fem* anglicized forms of **Sile**; variant forms are **Sheelagh, Sheelah**.

Sheldon *masc* a surname, meaning heathery hill with a shed, flat-topped hill, or steep valley, used as a first name (*Old English*).

Shelley *fem* a surname, meaning clearing on a bank, used as a firrst name (*Old English*).

Shepard *masc* a surname, meaning sheep herder, shepherd, used as a first name (*Old English*).

Sherborne, Sherbourne *masc* a surname, meaning clear stream, used as a first name (*Old English*).

Sheree, Sheri *fem* variant forms of **Chérie**.

Sheridan *masc* a surname, meaning seeking, used as a first name (*Irish Gaelic*).

Sherlock *masc* fair-haired (*Old English*).

Sherman *masc* a surname, meaning shearman, used as a first name (*Old English*).

Sherwin *masc* a surname, meaning loyal friend or fast-footed, used as a first name (*Old English*).

Sherwood *masc* a placename and surname, meaning

shore wood, used as a first name (*Old English*).

Sheryl *fem* a variant form of **Cheryl**.

Shirley *fem* a surname and placename, meaning thin clearing, used as a first name; a diminutive form is **Shirl**.

Sholto *masc* sower, seed-bearing (*Scots Gaelic*).

Shona *fem* the anglicized form of **Seonaid**.

Sian *fem* the Welsh form of **Jane**.

Sibeal *fem* an Irish form of **Sybyl**.

Sibyl, Sibylla *fem* variant forms of **Sybyl, Sybylla**; a diminutive form is **Sib**.

Siddall, Siddell *masc* a surname, meaning broad slope, used as a first name (*Old English*).

Sidney *masc fem* a surname, meaning wide island, used as a first name; a variant form is **Sydney**; a diminutive form is **Sid**.

Sidonia, Sidonie, Sydony *fem* from Sidon (*Latin*).

Siegfried *masc* victory and peace (*Germanic*).

Siegmund *masc* the German form of **Sigmund**.

Sierra *fem* the name for a mountain range used as a first name (*Spanish*).

Sigismond *masc* the French form of **Sigmund**.

Sigismondo *masc* the Italian form of **Sigmund**.

Sigiswald *masc* victorious ruler (*Germanic*).

Sigmund *masc* conquering protection (*Germanic*); a diminutive form is **Sig**.

Sigrid *fem* fair and victorious (*Old Norse*); a diminutive form is **Siri**.

Sigurd *masc* victorious guardian (*Old Norse*).

Silas *masc* a shortened form of **Silvanus**.

Sile *fem* the Gaelic form of **Celia, Cecily**, often rendered in English as **Sheila, Shelagh**, etc.

Silvain *masc* a French form of **Silvanus**.

Silvana *fem* form of **Silvano**.

Silvano *masc* the Italian form of **Silvanus**.

Silvanus *masc* of the woods (*Latin*); a variant form is **Sylvanus**.

Silvester *masc* bred in the country; rustic (*Latin*); a variant form is **Sylvester**; a diminutive form is **Sly**.

Silvestre *masc* a French and Spanish form of **Silvester**.

Silvestro *masc* an Italian form of **Silvester**.

Silvia *fem* of the woods (*Latin*); a variant form is **Sylvia**.

Silvie *fem* the French form of **Silvia**.

Silvio *masc* the Italian and Spanish forms of **Silvanus**.

Sim *masc* a diminutive form of **Simon, Simeon**; *fem* a diminutive form of **Simone**.

Simon, Simeon *masc* hearing with acceptance (*Hebrew*); diminutive forms are **Sim, Simmy**.

Simona *fem* form of **Simon**; a diminutive form is **Sim**.

Simone *fem* the French form of **Simona**.

Sinclair *masc* a surname, meaning from St Clair in France, used as a first name (*Old French*); a variant form is **St Clair**.

Sine *fem* a Gaelic form of **Jane**, often rendered in English as **Sheena**.

Sinead *fem* an Irish Gaelic form of **Janet**.

Siobhan *fem* an Irish Gaelic form of **Jane**.

Sioned *fem* a Welsh form of **Janet**.

Sisley *fem* a variant form of **Cecily**; diminutive forms are **Sis, Sissie, Sissy**.

Siwald *masc* a variant form of **Sewald**.

Skelton *masc* a surname, meaning farmstead on a hill, used as first name (*Old English*).

Skerry *masc* sea rock (*Old Norse*).

Skipper *masc* a nickname and surname, meaning jumping (Middle English) or ship's captain (*Dutch*), used as a first name; a diminutive form is **Skip**.

Skipton *masc* a placename and surname, meaning sheep farm, used as a first name (*Old English*).

Slade *masc* a surname, meaning valley, used as a first name (*Old English*).

Sly *masc* a diminutive form of **Silvester, Sylvester**.

Smith *masc* a surname, meaning blacksmith, used as a first name (*Old English*).

Snowden, Snowdon *masc* a surname, meaning snowy hill, used as a first name (*Old English*).

Sofie *fem* the French form of **Sophie**.

Sol *masc* the sun (*Latin*); a diminutive form of **Solomon**.

Solly *masc* a diminutive form of **Solomon**.

Solomon *masc* peaceable (*Hebrew*); diminutive forms are **Sol, Solly**.

Solveig *fem* house strong (*Old Norse*).

Somerled *masc* summer traveller (*Old Norse*).

Somerset *masc* a placename, meaning settlers around

the summer farmstead, used as a first name (*Old English*).

Somerton *masc* a placename, meaning summer farmstead, used as a first name (*Old English*).

Somhairle *masc* an Irish and Scots Gaelic form of **Somerled**.

Sonya, Sonia *fem* a Russian diminutive form of **Sophia**.

Sophia *fem* wisdom (*Greek*).

Sophie, Sophy *fem* diminutive forms of **Sophia**, now used independently.

Sophronia *fem* of a sound mind (*Greek*).

Sorcha *fem* bright one (*Irish Gaelic*).

Sorley *masc* an anglicized form of **Somhairle**.

Sorrel *masc* sour (*Germanic*), the name of a salad plant used as a first name.

Spencer *masc* a surname, meaning steward, butler or dispenser, used as a first name (*Old French*).

Spring *fem* desire (*Sanskrit*), the name of the season between winter and summer used as a first name.

Squire *masc* a surname, meaning shield bearer, used as a first name (*Old French*).

Stacey *masc* a diminutive form of **Eustace**, now used independently; *fem* a diminutive form of **Eustacia, Anastasia**, now used independently.

Stacy, Stacie *fem* diminutive forms of **Eustacia, Anastasia**, now used independently.

Stafford *masc* a surname, meaning ford by a landing place, used as a first name (*Old English*).

Stamford *masc* a variant form of **Stanford**.

Standish *masc* a surname, meaning stony pasture, used as a first name (*Old English*).

Stanford *masc* a surname, meaning stone ford, used as a first name (*Old English*); a variant form is **Stamford**.

Stanhope *masc* a surname, meaning stony hollow, used as a first name (*Old English*).

Stanislas, Stanislaus *masc* government and glory (*Slavonic*).

Stanley *masc* a surname and placename meaning stony field, used as a first name (*Old English*).

Stanton *masc* a surname, meaning stony farmstead, used as first name (*Old English*).

Star, Starr *fem* an English form of **Stella**.

Stasia *fem* a diminutive form of **Anastasia**.

Stefan *masc* a German form of **Stephen**.

Stefano *masc* the Italian form of **Stephen**.

Steffi, Steffie *fem* diminutive forms of **Stephanie**.

Stella *fem* a star (*Latin*).

Stephan *masc* a German form of **Stephen**.

Stephanie *fem* form of **Stephen**; a diminutive form is **Stevie**.

Stephen, Steven *masc* a crown or garland (*Greek*); diminutive forms are **Steve, Stevie**.

Sterling *masc* a surname, meaning little star, used as a first name (*Old English*); a variant form is **Stirling**.

Stewart *masc* a variant and surname form of **Stuart**.

Stirling *masc* a variant form of **Sterling**; a placename, meaning enclosed land by the stream, used as a first name (*Scottish Gaelic*).

St John *masc* Saint John (pronounced *sinjon*).

Stockland *masc* a surname, meaning land of a religious house, used as a first name (*Old English*).

Stockley *masc* a surname, meaning cleared meadow of a religious house, used as a first name (*Old English*).

Stockton *masc* a placename and surname, meaning outlying farmstead, used as a first name (*Old English*).

Stoddard *masc* a surname, meaning horse keeper, used as a first name (*Old English*).

Stoke *masc* a placename and surname, meaning outlying farmstead, used as a first name (*Old English*).

Storm *masc, fem* the word for a meteorological condition of violent winds and rain, hail or snow used as a first name (*Old English*).

Stowe *masc* a surname, meaning holy place, used as a first name (*Old English*).

Strachan, Strahan *masc* a surname, meaning littl valley, used as a first name (*Scots Gaelic*).

Stratford *masc* a placename, meaning ford on a Roman road, used as a first name (*Old English*).

Stuart, Stewart, Steuart *masc* the surname meaning "steward" used as a first name (*Old English*).

Sukey, Sukie *fem* diminutive forms of **Susan**.

Sullivan *masc* a surname, meaning black-eyed, used as a surname (*Irish Gaelic*).

Summer *fem* season (*Sanskrit*), the name of the season between spring and autumn used as a personal name.

Sumner *masc* a surname, meaning one who summons, used as a first name (*Old French*).

Susan *fem* the English form of **Susanna**; diminutive forms are **Sue, Sukey, Sukie, Susie, Susy**.

Susanna, Susannah *fem* a lily (*Hebrew*); a variant form is **Suzanna**.

Susanne *fem* a German form of **Susanna**.

Sutherland *masc* a placename and surname, meaning southern land, used as a first name (*Old Norse*).

Sutton *masc* a placename and surname, meaning southern farmstead, used as a first name (*Old English*).

Suzanna *fem* a variant form of **Susanna**.

Suzanne *fem* a French and German form of **Susan**.

Sven *masc* lad (*Old Norse*).

Sybille *fem* the French form of **Sybyl**.

Sybyl, Sybilla *fem* a prophetess (*Greek*); variant forms are **Sibyl, Sibylla**; a diminutive form is **Syb**.

Sydney *masc* a variant form of **Sidney**.

Sylvain *masc* a French form of **Silvanus**.

Sylvanus *masc* a variant form of **Silvanus**.

Sylvester *masc* a variant form of **Silvester**; a diminutive form is **Sly**.

Sylvia *fem* a variant form of **Silvia**.

Sylvie *fem* the French form of **Silvia**.

T

Tabitha *fem* a gazelle (*Aramaic*); diminutive forms are **Tab, Tabby**.

Tad *masc* a diminutive form of **Thaddeus**, also used independently.

Taddeo *masc* the Italian form of **Thaddeus**.

Tadhg *masc* an Irish Gaelic form of **Thaddeus**; a variant form is **Teague**.

Taffy *masc* Welsh form of David (*Celtic*).

Taggart *masc* a surname, meaning priest, used as a first name (*Scots Gaelic*).

Tate *masc* a surname, meaning cheerful, used as a first name (*Old Norse*); variant forms are **Tait, Teyte**.

Talbot *masc* a surname, meaning command of the valley, used as a first name (*Germanic*).

Talitha *fem* maiden (*Aramaic*).

Tallulah *fem* a placename, meaning spring water, used as a first name (*North American Indian*).

Tam *masc Scots* a diminutive form of **Thomas**.

Tamar *fem* date palm (*Hebrew*); diminutive forms are **Tammie, Tammy**.

Tamara *fem* the Russian form of **Tamar**.

Tammie, Tammy *fem* diminutive forms of **Tamar, Tamsin**; *masc* a diminutive form of **Thomas**.

Tamsin *fem* a Cornish contraction of **Thomasina**, now used independently; a diminutive form is **Tammie**.

Tancredi *masc* an Italian form of **Tancredo**.

Tancredo *masc* thoughtful, deliberative (*Germanic*).

Tania, Tanya *fem* diminutive forms of **Tatiana, Titania**, now used independently.

Tanisha *fem* born on Monday (*Hausa*).

Tansy *fem* immortal (*Greek*), the name of a medicinal plant bearing yellow flowers used as a first name.

Tara *fem* a placename, meaning rocky assembly place, used as a first name; in Irish history, the site of ancient royal power (*Irish Gaelic*).

Tate *masc* a variant form of **Tait**.

Tatiana *fem* form of a Roman family name of unknown meaning (*Latin*); diminutive forms are **Tania, Tanya**.

Taylor *masc* a surname, meaning tailor, used as a first name (*Old French*).

Teague *masc* a variant form of **Tadhg**.

Tebaldo *masc* an Italian form of **Theobold**.

Ted, Teddie, Teddy *masc* diminutive forms of **Edward, Theodore, Theodoric**.

Tempest *fem* the word for a violent storm used as a first name (*Latin*).

Tennison, Tennyson *masc* variant forms of **Dennison**.

Teobaldo *masc* an Italian and Spanish form of **Theobald**.

Teodorico *masc* an Italian form of **Theodoric**.

Teodoro *masc* an Italian and Spanish form of **Theodore**.

Teodora *fem* an Italian and Spanish form of **Theodora**.

Teodosia *fem* an Italian form of **Theodosia**.

Terence *masc* from a Roman family name of unknown origin (*Latin*); variant forms are **Terrance, Terrence**; diminutive forms are **Tel, Terry**.

Terencio *masc* a Spanish form of **Terence**.

Teresa *fem* the Italian and Spanish forms of **Theresa**.

Terese *fem* a variant form of **Theresa**.

Teri *fem* a diminutive form of **Theresa**.

Terrance, Terrence *masc* variant forms of **Terence**.

Terri *fem* a diminutive form of **Teresa, Theresa**, now used independently.

Terris, Terriss *masc* a surname, meaning son of Terence, used as a first name.

Terry *fem* a diminutive form of **Teresa**; *masc* a diminutive form of **Terence**.

Tertius *masc* third born (*Latin*).

Tess, Tessa, Tessie *fem* diminutive forms of **Esther, Teresa, Theresa**.

Teyte *masc* a variant form of **Tait**.

Thaddeus *masc* gift of God (*Greek-Aramaic*); diminutive forms are **Tad, Thad, Thaddy**.

Thaine *masc* a surname, meaning holder of land in return for military service, used as a first name (*Old English*); a variant form is **Thane**.

Thalia *fem* flourishing blossom (*Greek*).

Thane *masc* a variant form of **Thaine**.

Thea *fem* a diminutive form of **Althea, Dorothea**, now used independently.

Thecla *fem* god glory (*Greek*).

Thelma *fem* will (*Greek*).

Theda *fem* a diminutive form of **Theodora, Theodosia**.

Thelma *fem* a name coined in the 19th century by Marie Corelli for her novel *Thelma*, perhaps from wish (*Greek*).

Theo *masc fem* diminutive forms of **Theobald, Theodore, Theodora**.

Theobald *masc* bold for the people (*Germanic*); a diminutive form is **Theo**.

Theodor *masc* a Scandinavian and German form of **Theodore**.

Theodora *fem* form of **Theodore**; diminutive forms are **Dora, Theo**.

Theodore *masc* the gift of God (*Greek*); diminutive forms are **Ted, Teddie, Teddy, Theo**.

Theodoric, Theodorick *masc* ruler of the people (*Germanic*); diminutive forms are **Derek, Derrick, Dirk, Ted, Teddie, Teddy**.

Theodorus *masc* a Dutch form of **Theodore**.

Theodosia *fem* the gift of God (*Greek*).

Theodosius *masc* form of **Theodosia**.

Theophila *fem* form of **Theophilus**.

Theophilus *masc* a lover of God (*Greek*).

Theresa *fem* carrying ears of corn (*Greek*); diminutive forms are **Teri, Terri, Terry, Tess, Tessa, Tessie, Tracey, Tracie, Tracy**.

Thérèse *fem* the French form of **Theresa**.

Theresia, Therese *fem* German forms of **Theresa**.

Theron *masc* a hero (*Greek*).

Thewlis *masc* a surname, meaning ill-mannered, used as a first name (*Old English*).

Thibaut *masc* a French form of **Theobald**.

Thierry *masc* a French form of **Theodoric**.

Thirza *fem* pleasantness (*Hebrew*); variant forms are **Thyrza, Tirza**.

Thomas *masc* a twin (*Aramaic*); diminutive forms are **Tam, Thom, Tom, Tommy**.

Thomasina, Thomasine *fem* forms of **Thomas**.

Thor *masc* thunder (Old Norse), in Norse mythology, the god of thunder; a variant form is **Tor**.

Thora *fem* form of **Thor**.

Thorburn *masc* a surname, meaning Thor's warrior or bear, used as a first name (*Old Norse*).

Thordis *fem* a variant form of **Tordis**.

Thorndike, Thorndyke *masc* a surname, meaning thorny ditch, used as a first name (*Old English*).

Thorne *masc* a surname, meaning thorn tree or hawthorn, used as a first name (*Old English*).

Thorold *masc* Thor ruler (Old Norse); a variant form is **Torold**.

Thorp, Thorpe *masc* a surname, meaning farm village,

used as a first name (*Old English*).

Thorwald *masc* ruled by Thor (*Old Norse*); a variant form is **Torvald**.

Thurstan, Thurston *masc* a surname, meaning Thor's stone, used as a first name (*Old Norse*).

Thyrza *fem* a variant form of **Thirza**.

Tib, Tibbie *fem Scots* diminutive forms of **Isabel, Isabella**.

Tibold *masc* a German form of **Theobald**.

Tiebout *masc* a Dutch form of **Theobald**.

Tiernan, Tierney *masc* a surname, meaning lord, used as a first name (*Irish Gaelic*); a variant form is **Kiernan**.

Tiffany *fem* the manifestation of God, the festival of Epiphany (*Greek*).

Tilda, Tilde *fem* diminutive forms of **Matilda**.

Till *masc* a German diminutive form of Dietrich.

Tilly *fem* a diminutive form of **Matilda**.

Tim *masc* a diminutive form of **Timon, Timothy**.

Timon *masc* reward (*Greek*).

Timothea *fem* form of **Timothy**.

Timothy *masc* honouring God (*Greek*); diminutive forms are **Tim, Timmie, Timmy**.

Tina *fem* a diminutive form of **Christina, Christine**, etc, also used independently.

Tiphaine *fem* a French form of **Tiffany**.

Tiree *fem* the name of an island, meaning land of corn, used as a first name (*Scots Gaelic*).

Tirza, Tirzah *fem* variant forms of **Thirza**.

Tita *fem* form of **Titus**; a diminutive form of **Martita**.

Titania *fem* giant, in medieval folklore wife of Oberon and queen of fairies (*Greek*); diminutive forms are **Tania, Tanya**.

Titian *masc* an English form of **Titianus**.

Titianus *masc* a Roman name derived from **Titus**.

Tito *masc* the Italian and Spanish form of **Titus**.

Titus *masc* of uncertain meaning, possibly infantile (*Latin*)

Tiziano *masc* the Italian form of **Titianus**.

Tobey *fem* form of **Toby**; a variant form is **Tobi**.

Tobi *masc* a variant form of **Toby**; *fem* a variant form of **Tobey**.

Tobias, Tobiah *masc* distinguished of the Lord (*Hebrew*); a diminutive form is **Toby**.

Toby *masc* a diminutive form of **Tobias**, now used independently; a variant form is **Tobi**.

Todd *masc* a surname, meaning fox, used as a first name (*Old Norse*).

Todhunter *masc* a surname, meaning foxhunter, used as a first name (*Old Norse/Old English*).

Tom *masc* a diminutive form of **Thomas**, now used independently.

Tomas *masc* the Spanish form of **Thomas**.

Tomasina, Tomina *fem* forms of **Thomas**.

Tomás *masc* a Spanish form of **Thomas**.

Tomaso, Tommaso *masc* Italian forms of **Thomas**.

Tommaso *masc* an Italian form of **Thomas**.

Tommie, Tommy *masc* diminutive forms of **Thomas**.

Toni *fem* diminutive forms of **Annette, Antoinette, Antonia**, now used independently.

Tonia *fem* a diminutive form of **Antonia**.

Tonie *fem* diminutive forms of **Annette, Antoinette, Antonia**, now used independently.

Tony *masc* a diminutive form of **Antony**; *fem* a diminutive form of **Annette, Antoinette, Antonia**.

Topaz *fem* the name of a white gemstone used as a first name topaz gem.

Tordis *fem* Thor's goddess (*Old Norse*); a variant form is **Thordis**.

Tormod *masc* Thor's spirit (*Old Norse*).

Torold *masc* a variant form of **Thorold**.

Torquil *masc* god's cauldron (*Old Norse*).

Tor *masc* a variant form of **Thor**.

Torr *masc* a surname, meaning tower (*Old English*) or bull (*Old French*) used as a first name.

Torvald *masc* a variant form of **Thorwald**.

Tory *fem* a diminutive form of **Victoria**.

Townsend, Townshend *masc* a surname, meaning end of the village, used as a first name (*Old English*).

Tracey *masc* a variant form of **Tracy**; *fem* a diminutive form of **Teresa, Theresa**.

Tracie *fem* a diminutive form of **Teresa, Theresa**, now used independently.

Tracy *masc* a surname, meaning Thracian, used as a first name (*Old French*); a variant form is **Tracey**; *fem* a diminutive form of **Teresa, Theresa**, now used independently.

Traherne *masc* a surname, meaning iron strength, used as a first name (*Welsh*).

Travers *masc* a surname, meaning crossing, crossroads, used as a first name (*Old French*); a variant form is **Travis**.

Traviata *fem* lead astray, the title of Verdi's opera used as a first name (*Italian*).

Travis *masc* a variant form of **Travers**.

Tremaine, Tremayne *masc* a surname, meaning homestead on the rock, used as a first name (*Cornish*).

Trent *masc* a river name, meaning liable to flood, used as a first name (*Celtic*).

Trev *masc* a diminutive form of **Trevor**.

Trevelyan *masc* a surname, meaning mill farm, used as a first name (*Cornish*).

Trevor *masc* a surname, meaning big river, used as a first name (*Welsh*); a diminutive form is **Trev**.

Tricia *fem* a diminutive form of **Patricia**.

Trilby *fem* a name coined by George du Maurier in the 19th century for the heroine of his novel *Trilby*.

Trisha *fem* a diminutive form of **Patricia**.

Tristram, Tristam, Tristan *masc* grave; pensive (*Latin*); tumult (*Celtic*).

Trix, Trixie *fem* diminutive forms of **Beatrice**.

Troy *masc* a surname, meaning of Troyes, used as a first name (*Old French*); the name of the city in Asia Minor besieged by the Greeks used as a first name.

Truda, Trudie, Trudy *fem* diminutive forms of **Gertrude**.

True *masc* the adjective for the quality of being faithful and loyal used as a first name.

Truelove *masc* a surname, meaning faithful sweetheart, used as a first name (*Old English*).

Trueman, Truman *masc* a surname, meaning faithful servant, used as a first name (*Old English*).

Trystan *masc* a Welsh form of **Tristan**.

Tudor *masc* a Welsh form of **Theodore**.

Tuesday *fem* day of Mars (Old English), the name of the second day of the week used as a first name (*Old English*).

Tullio *masc* the Italian form of **Tullius**.

Tullius *masc* a Roman family name of Etruscan origin and uncertain meaning.

Tully *masc* a surname, meaning flood, used as a first name (*Irish Gaelic*); an English form of **Tullius**.

Turner *masc* a surname, meaning worker on a lathe, used as a first name (*Old French*).

Turpin *masc* a surname, meaning Thor the Finn, used as a first name (*Old Norse*).

Twyford *masc* a surname, meaning double ford, used as a first name (*Old English*).

Ty *masc* a diminutive form of **Tybalt, Tyler, Tyrone, Tyson**.

Tybalt *masc* a variant form of **Theobald**; a diminutive form is **Ty**.

Tye *masc* a surname, meaning enclosure, used as a first name (*Old English*).

Tyler *masc* a surname, meaning tile-maker, used as a first name (*Old English*); a diminutive form is **Ty**.

Tyrone *masc* a placename and surname, meaning land of Owen, used as a first name (*Irish Gaelic*); a diminutive form is **Ty**.

Tyson *masc* a surname, meaning firebrand, used as a first name (*Old French*); a diminutive form is **Ty**.

U

Uberto *masc* an Italian form of **Hubert**.

Uda *fem* form of **Udo**.

Udo *masc* prosperous (*Germanic*).

Udall, Udell *masc* a surname, meaning yew-tree valley, used as a first name (*Old English*).

Ugo, Ugolino, Ugone *masc* Italian forms of **Hugh**.

Ulises *masc* a Spanish form of **Ulysses**.

Ulisse *masc* an Italian form of **Ulysses**.

Ulmar, Ulmer *masc* wolf (*Old English*).

Ulric, Ulrick *masc* wolf power (*Old English*); the English form of **Ulrich**.

Ulrica *fem* English form of **Ulrike**.

Ulrich *masc* fortune and power (*Germanic*).

Ulrike *fem* form of **Ulrich**.

Ulysses *masc* a hater (*Greek*)—*dimin* **Lyss**.

Umberto *masc* the Italian form of **Humbert**.

Una *fem* a lamb; hunger (*Irish Gaelic*); *fem* form of one (*Latin*) used by Edmund Spenser in *The Faerie Queene*.

Unity *fem* the quality of harmony or concord used as a first name.

Unwin

Unwin *masc* a surname, meaning not a friend, used as a surname (*Old English*).

Upton *masc* a surname, meaning upper farmstead, used as a first name (*Old English*).

Urania *fem* heavenly—the name of one of the muses (*Greek*).

Urbaine *masc* the French form of **Urban**.

Urban *masc* of the town, courteous; polished (*Latin*).

Urbano *masc* the Italian form of **Urban**.

Uri *masc* light (*Hebrew*).

Uriah *masc* fire of the Lord (*Hebrew*).

Urian *masc* a husbandman (*Danish*).

Uriel *masc* light of God (*Hebrew*).

Ursula *fem* she-bear (*Latin*).

Ursule *fem* the French form of **Ursula**.

Uzziah *masc* Jehovah is strength (*Hebrew*).

Uzziel *masc* God is strength (*Hebrew*).

V

Vachel *masc* little cow (*Old French*).

Vail *masc* a surname, meaning valley, used as a first name (*Old English*).

Val *masc* a diminutive form of **Valentine**; *fem* a diminutive form of **Valentina, Valerie**.

Valborga *fem* Protecting ruler (*Germanic*); diminutive forms are **Walburga, Walborga, Valburga**.

Valdemar *masc* a variant form of **Waldemar**.

Valdemaro *masc* an Italian form of **Waldemar**.

Valentin *masc* a French, German and Scandinavian form of **Valentine**.

Valentina *fem* form of **Valentine**; a diminutive form is **Val**.

Valentine *masc fem* strong; healthy; powerful (*Latin*); a diminutive form is **Val**.

Valentino *masc* an Italian form of **Valentine**.

Valerian *masc* form of **Valerie**.

Valeriano *masc* an Italian form of **Valerian**.

Valerie *fem* healthy, strong (*Latin*); a diminutive form is **Val**.

Valerio *masc* an Italian form of **Valerian**.

Valéry *masc* foreign power (*Germanic*).

Van *masc* from, of, a prefix in Dutch surnames now used independently as an English-language first name.

Vance *masc* young (*Old English*).

Vanessa *fem* a name invented by Jonathan Swift for his friend Esther Vanhomrigh, created from the prefix of her surname plus the suffix *essa*; a diminutive form is **Nessa**.

Vasili, Vassily *masc* Russian forms of **Basil**.

Vaughan, Vaughn *masc* a surname, meaning small one, used as a first name (*Welsh*).

Velvet *fem* the English name of a rich, soft cloth used as a first name .

Venetia *fem* the name of the region around Venice in northern Italy used as a first name (*Latin*).

Vera *fem* faith (*Russian*); true (*Latin*).

Vere *masc* a surname, meaning from Ver in France, used as a first name (*Old French*).

Vergil *masc* a variant form of **Virgil**.

Verity *fem* truth (*Latin*).

Verne, Verna *fem* diminutive forms of **Laverne**.

Vernon *masc* a surname, meaning alder tree, used as a first name (*Old French*).

Verona *fem* a variant form of **Veronica**.

Veronica *fem* true image (*Latin*); a variant form is **Verona**; diminutive forms are **Ronnie, Ronny**.

Veronika *fem* a Scandinavian form of **Veronica**.

Veronike *fem* a German form of **Veronica**.

Véronique *fem* a French form of **Veronica**.

Vesta *fem* of uncertain meaning; in Roman mythology, the goddess of the hearth (*Latin*).

Vi *fem* a diminutive form of **Viola, Violet**.

Vicente *masc* a Spanish form of **Vincent**.

Vicki, Vickie, Vicky *fem* a diminutive form of **Victoria**, now used independently.

Victoire *fem* a French form of **Victoria**.

Victor *masc* a conqueror (*Latin*); a diminutive form is **Vic**.

Victoria *fem* victory (*Latin*); diminutive forms are **Tory, Vickie, Vita**.

Vidal *masc* a Spanish form of *vitalis* (*Latin*), living vital.

Vilhelm *masc* a Swedish form of **William**.

Vilhelmina *fem* a Swedish form of **Wilhelmina**.

Vilma *fem* a diminutive form of **Vilhelmina**.

Vincent *masc* conquering; victorious (*Latin*); diminutive forms are **Vince, Vinnie, Vinny**.

Vincente *masc* an Italian form of **Vincent**.

Vincentia *fem* form of **Vincent**.

Vincenz *masc* a German form of **Vincent**.

Vinnie, Vinny *masc* diminutive forms of **Vincent**.

Vinson *masc* a surname form of **Vincent** used as a first name (*Old English*).

Viola, Violet *fem* a violet (*Latin*); a diminutive form is **Vi**.

Violetta *fem* the Italian form of **Viola, Violet**.

Virgil *masc* staff bearer (*Latin*), the name of the Roman poet of the first century BC; a variant form is **Vergil**.

Virgilio *masc* the Italian and Spanish form of **Virgil**.

Virginia *fem* virgin; pure (*Latin*); a diminutive form is **Ginnie**.

Virginie *fem* a Dutch and French form of **Virginia**.

Vita *fem* form of **Vito**; a diminutive form of **Victoria**.

Vitale *masc* an Italian form of *vitalis* (*Latin*), living, vital.

Vito *masc* the Italian form of **Vitus**.

Vitore *masc* an Italian form of **Victor**.

Vitoria *fem* a Spanish form of **Victoria**.

Vitorio *masc* the Spanish form of **Victor**.

Vittorio *masc* an Italian form of **Victor**.

Vitus *masc* life (*Latin*).

Viv *fem* a diminutive form of **Vivien**.

Vivian, Vyvian *masc* lively (Latin); a variant form is **Vyvian**.

Vivien, Vivienne *fem* form of **Vivian**; a diminutive form is **Viv**.

Vladimir *masc* Royally famous. A renowned monarch (*Slavic*).

Vladislav *masc* great ruler (*Slavonic*).

Vyvian *masc* a variant form of **Vivian**.

W

Wade *masc* a surname, meaning to go, or at the ford, used as a first name (*Old English*).

Wadsworth *masc* a surname, meaning Wade's homestead, used as a first name (*Old English*); a variant form is **Wordsworth**.

Wainwright *masc* a surname, meaning maker of carts, used as a first name (*Old English*).

Wake *masc* a surname, meaning alert, watchful, used as a first name (*Old English*).

Waldo *masc* ruler (*Germanic*).

Waldemar *masc* noted ruler (*Germanic*); a variant form is **Valdemar**.

Walker *masc* a surname, meaning a fuller, used as a first name (*Old English*).

Wallace *masc* a Scots variant form of **Wallis**; a diminutive form is **Wally**.

Wallis *masc fem* a surname, meaning foreigner, used as a first name (*Old French*); a variant form is **Wallace**; a diminutive form is **Wally**.

Wally *masc* a diminutive form of **Wallace, Wallis**.

Walt masc a diminutive form of **Walter, Walton**.

Walter

Walter *masc* rule army/people (*Germanic*); diminutive forms are **Walt, Wat, Watty**.

Walther *masc* a German form of **Walter**.

Walton *masc* a surname, meaning farmstead of the Britons, used as a first name (*Old English*); a diminutive form is **Walt**.

Wanda *fem* a variant form of **Wenda**.

Ward *masc* a surname, meaning watchman; guard, used as a first name (*Old English*).

Warfield *masc* a surname, meaning field of the stream of the wrens, used as a first name (*Old English*).

Warne *masc* a surname, meaning alder wood, used as a first name (*Cornish*).

Warner *masc* a surname, meaning protecting army, used as a first name (*Germanic*).

Warren *masc* a surname, meaning wasteland or game park, used as a first name (*Old French*).

Warwick *masc* a placename and surname, meaning dwellings by the weir, used as a first name (*Old English*).

Washington *masc* a surname, meaning Wassa's estate, used as a first name (*Old English*).

Wat, Watty *masc* a diminutive form of **Walter**.

Waverley *masc* a placename, meaning meadow or clearing by the swampy ground, used as a first name (*Old English*).

Wayne *masc* a surname, meaning a carter, used as a first name.

Webb *masc* a surname, meaning weaver, used as a first name (*Old English*).

Webster *masc* a surname, meaning woman weaver, used as a first name (*Old English*).

Wellington *masc* a placename and surname, meaning Weola's farmstead, used as a first name (*Old English*).

Wenceslaus, Wenceslas *masc* wreathed with glory (*Slavonic*).

Wenda *fem* form of **Wendel**; a variant form is **Wanda**.

Wendel, Wendell *masc* of the Wend people (*Germanic*); a variant form is **Wendel**.

Wendy *fem* invented by J. M. Barrie for the main female character in his play *Peter Pan*.

Wentworth *masc* a surname, meaning winter enclosure, used as a first name (*Old English*).

Werner *masc* a German form of **Warner**.

Wesley *masc* a surname, meaning west wood, made famous by the Methodists John and Charles Wesley, used as a first name (*Old English*); a diminutive form is **Wes**.

Whitaker *masc* a surname, meaning white acre, used as a first name (*Old English*); a variant form is **Whittaker**.

Whitman *masc* a surname, meaning white- or fair-haired, used as a first name (*Old English*).

Whitney *masc, fem* a surname and placename, meaning white island or Witta's island, used as a first name (*Old English*).

Whittaker *masc* a variant form of **Whitaker**.

Wilbert *masc* well-born (*Old English*).

Wilbur *masc* resolute fortress (*Old English*).

Wilfrida, Wilfreda *fem* form of **Wilfrid**.

Wilfrid, Wilfred *masc* resolute peace (*Germanic*); a diminutive form is **Wilf**.

Wilhelm *masc* the German form of **William**; a diminutive form is **Wim**.

Wilhelmina, Wilhelmine *fem* form of **Wilhelm**; diminutive forms are **Elma, Minna, Minnie, Wilma**.

Will, Willie, Willy *masc* diminutive forms of **William**.

Willa *fem* form of **Will, William**.

Willard *masc* a surname, meaning bold resolve, used as a first name (*Old English*).

Willemot *masc* resolute in spirit (*Germanic*).

William *masc* resolute helmet or helmet of resolution; defence; protector (*Germanic*); diminutive forms are **Bill, Will**.

Williamina *fem* form of **William**.

Willoughby *masc* a surname, meaning farm by the willows, used as a first name (*Old Norse/Old English*).

Willson *masc* a variant form of **Wilson**.

Wilma *fem* a diminutive form of **Wilhelmina**; *fem* form of **William**.

Wilmer *masc* famous will or desire (*Old English*); *masc* form of **Wilma**.

Wilmot *masc* a diminutive surname form of **William** used as a first name.

Wilson masc a surname, meaning son of Will, used as a first name (*Old English*); a variant form is **Willson**.

Wilton *masc* a placename and surname, meaning floodable place, used as a first name (*Old English*).

Wim *masc* a contraction of **Wilhelm**.

Windham *masc* a variant form of **Wyndham**.

Windsor *masc* a placename and surname, meaning slope with a windlass, used as a first name (*Old English*).

Winifred *fem* joy and peace (*Old English*); diminutive forms are **Freda, Win, Winnie, Wynn, Wynne**.

Winslow *masc* a placename and surname, meaning Wine's burial mound, used as a first name (*Old English*).

Winston *masc* a placename and surname, meaning friend's place or farm, used as a first name (*Old English*).

Winter *masc* the name for the cold season of the year used as a first name (*Old English*).

Winthrop *masc* a surname, meaning friend's farm village, used as a first name(*Old English*).

Winton *masc* a surname, meaning friend's farm, used as a first name (*Old English*).

Wolf, Wolfe *masc* wolf (*Old English*).

Wolfgang *masc* bold wolf (*Germanic*).

Wolfram *masc* wolf raven (*Germanic*).

Woodrow *masc* a surname, meaning row (of houses) in a wood, used as a first name; a diminutive form is **Woody**.

Woodward *masc* a surname, meaning forest guardian, used as a first name (*Old English*).

Woody *masc* a diminutive form of **Woodrow**, now used independently.

Wordsworth *masc* a variant form of **Wadsworth**.

Worth *masc* a surname, meaning farmstead, used as a first name (*Old English*).

Wyman *masc* a surname, meaning battle protector, used as a first name (*Old English*).

Wyn *masc* white (*Welsh*); a variant form is **Wynn**.

Wyndham *masc* a surname, meaning homestead of Wyman, used as a first name (*Old English*); a variant form is **Windham**.

Wynn, Wynne *masc*, *fem* a surname, meaning friend, used as a first name; *masc* a variant form of **Wyn**; *fem* a diminutive form of **Winifred**.

X

Xanthe *fem* yellow (*Greek*).

Xavier *masc* a placename, meaning new house owner, used as a first name (*Spanish/Basque*).

Xaviera *fem* form of **Xavier**.

Xena, Xene, Xenia *fem* hospitality (*Greek*).

Xenos *masc* stranger (*Greek*).

Xerxes *masc* royal (*Persian*).

Y

Yale *masc* a surname, meaning fertile upland (*Welsh*).

Yasmin, Yasmine *fem* variant forms of **Jasmine**.

Yehuda *fem* a variant form of **Jehuda**.

Yehudi *masc* a Jew (*Hebrew*).

Yolanda *fem* a variant form of **Viola**.

York, Yorke *masc* a placename and surname, meaning estate of Eburos or of the yew trees, used as a first name (*Celtic/Latin/Old English*).

Yseult *fem* an old French form of **Isolde**.

Yuri *masc* a Russian form of **George**.

Yves *masc* a yew tree (*French-Germanic*).

Yvette *fem* a diminutive form of Yves.

Yvonne *fem* form of **Yves**.

Z

Zabdiel *masc* gift of God (*Hebrew*).

Zabrina *fem* a variant form of **Sabrina**.

Zaccheus *masc* innocent; pure (*Hebrew*).

Zachary, Zachariah, Zacharias *masc* remembered of
  the Lord (*Hebrew*); diminutive forms are **Zach, Zack,
  Zak**.

Zadok *masc* righteous (*Hebrew*).

Zara *fem* flower (*Arabic*).

Zeb *masc* a diminutive form of **Zebadiah, Zebedee,
  Zebulun**.

Zebadiah, Zebedee *masc* gift of the Lord (*Hebrew*).

Zebulun *masc* exaltation (*Hebrew*); diminutive forms
  are **Lonny, Zeb**.

Zedekiah *masc* justice of the Lord (*Hebrew*); a diminutive form is **Zed**.

Zeke *masc* a diminutive form of **Ezekiel**.

Zelig *masc* a variant form of **Selig**.

Zelma *fem* a variant form of **Selma**.

Zenas *masc* gift of Zeus (*Greek*).

Zenobia *fem* having life from Zeus (*Greek*).

Zephaniah *masc* hid of the Lord (*Hebrew*); a diminutive form is **Zeph**.

Zinnia

Zinnia *fem* the name of a plant with brightly coloured flowers used as a first name, named after the German botanist J. G. Zinn.

Zoë, Zoe *fem* life (*Greek*).

COLLECT YOUR OWN UNUSUAL NAMES

_____   _____

_____   _____

_____   _____

_____   _____

_____   _____

_____   _____

_____   _____

_____   _____

_____   _____

_____   _____

Collect your own Unusual Names

_____   _____

_____   _____

_____   _____

_____   _____

_____   _____

_____   _____

_____   _____

_____   _____

_____   _____

_____   _____

_____   _____

_____   _____

Collect your own Unusual Names

_____   _____

_____   _____

_____   _____

_____   _____

_____   _____

_____   _____

_____   _____

_____   _____

_____   _____

_____   _____

_____   _____

_____   _____

_____   _____

_____   _____

_____   _____

_____   _____

_____   _____

_____   _____

_____   _____

_____   _____

_____   _____

_____   _____

_____   _____

_____   _____